Get
WalletWise

The Workbook

Proven and Powerful

Personal Finance and

Budgeting Tips for Finding Financial

Freedom and Living a Debt-Free Life

By

Ken Remsen

To the Students

of my Liberal Arts Math Class

Who Showed Me

What Was Really Happening

in The American Economy

Table of Contents

Get WalletWise The Workbook

Introduction

Introduction

"A wise person should have money in their head, but not in their heart." - Jonathan Swift

"Ken, do you think it is possible for me to reset my money habits and undo years of money missteps?" I hear this repeatedly during my financial coaching sessions. I tell my clients that with determination, discipline, and hard work, they can get out of debt and build a nest egg. The key is to spend less than you earn. This is common sense; however, in our complex world of money, many of us do not know where we stand financially. We have a hunch, but we are not working from a budget, we are not balancing our checkbook, and we are not reading our credit card statements. Everything financial is on autopilot because that may be the path of least resistance. The best way to spend less is to have a "Low Threshold for Excitement." Buy a car you can afford. Buy a house that is less than you can afford, etc. Introduce yourself to inexpensive fun. It is unnecessary to spend your hard-earned money on fun until you have paid off your debts and started saving for the future. *Get WalletWise, The Workbook* puts you in the driver's seat so you can create your best money "you" and secure your financial well-being.

Getting wallet wise is easier than it sounds. "Spend less, save more." To achieve this simple financial goal, you need a lot of courage, strength, determination, and hard work. The workbook will direct you with a mix of exercises that will encourage beneficial spending habits. Many motivational speakers claim it takes 66 days (9 weeks) to build a habit. This means you have to give it time. There is no immediate gratification here. We will start by adding good habits one-by-one.

It is important to have a positive attitude in life and a positive attitude about money. If you are arrogant, fearful, indifferent, or negligent with money, the consequences are predictable. If you have a positive, and respectful attitude toward money, then the *Get WalletWise, The Workbook* will help you achieve a positive money mindset. It doesn't matter which life season you're living in. You may be a young entrepreneur, a student struggling with loans, or an employee finding it difficult to manage your finances. This workbook will help you create positive spending habits.

Before the Global Financial Crises of 2007-2008, I taught a personal finance math class in high school. In those classes, I learned that there was a desire by the students to learn personal finance. In class, I created a mock car salesroom and split the students into two groups: salespeople and the customers. It was hilarious to see the transformation of normally shy students into confident negotiators. I taught them as I want to teach you: The Seven Most Important Words in Negotiation. *"Is that the best you can do?"* I promise these seven words will save hundreds or thousands of dollars, maybe more, depending on your situation. Not only did I teach them what to say but also how to say it, and whether to say the words while negotiating or even while walking away from the salesperson and heading for the door, ready to leave. If you cannot strike a deal, my next favorite seven-word phrase is, *"Let me know if your situation changes."* As it was occurring to their family, a student asked me about the meaning of foreclosure. Another student gave me the book, *Maxed Out*. Written just before the 2008 Financial Crises, this book showed me that the consumer finance world is more "dog eat dog" than I knew. The book and its movie tell the story of how consumer lending and credit card companies make oversized profits while bleeding customers dry. The movie introduced me to the concept of debt collection brokers! Adding this to the many stories of personal money struggles from my friends and family, I knew I should do something positive for you. I wrote a book for you about managing money.

Who is this financial workbook for?

I wrote this workbook for high school students, college graduates, house of worship small groups, young families starting out who have their lives in front of them, and anyone who does not possess basic money management skills. Avoid unpaid balances on your credit cards. Do not borrow personal loans to pay back credit card debt. Max out your company's 401k. At the end of the month, you should have more money than month. I want you to avoid frightening money debacles!

Everyone's financial literacy could use a boost. Believe me, I know. I have made many of the mistakes discussed in this book and learned many lessons in the "School of Hard Knocks." Many of the lessons were very difficult, but I would not trade those well-earned knocks for anything. That history gave me the knowledge and strength to sit down and write this book for you.

Fortunately, I also received friendly advice. A mentor told me, "It is best to learn from other people's mistakes." I heartily agree. From my personal experiences, I share my observations with you.

Are you in…?

1. The Trapped Class
2. The Treadmill Class
3. The Freedom Class

Writer Ramit Sethi invented this description of the present day American economic class structure. *Get WalletWise* shows you how to move from the Trapped and Treadmill Class to the Freedom Class.

One financial advisor told my father that dad's nest egg did not have enough money to qualify for his advice. Another "advisor" later sold him unsuitable financial products. This book is for people like you, who make their living driving for UBER, work in a hotel or restaurant, or have any type of hard-working job. Young people who are learning how the world works should read this book. This book is for the working-class poor, who have jobs, but along with 50% of Americans, have no net worth. They have no equity in their houses or cars and have unsecured debts (credit cards mostly) that exceed their assets. I have been there myself and gotten "over the wall." Now, I want to help you achieve financial security.

Why does the world need financial literacy?

Imagine living in a society where you have achieved a positive money mindset and learned the basic skills to be competently "manage" your money. How do you think life would be in that society? If you answered, "a society where everyone enjoys a balanced, healthier, and above all, happier life", then that's what it could look like. And that's my dream: to help people become financially literate enough to change the world!

Why this Financial Self-Help Book?

In an interview with the well-recognized business tycoon, Jamie Dimon (chairperson of JP Morgan Chase) declared that the citizens of our country are having two distinct experiences: half of Americans work for large thriving corporations, and the other half of Americans work in less stable industries. It's like a *Tale of Two Cities*. Dimon said, "It is absolutely obvious that a big chunk of (people) have been left behind. Forty percent of Americans make less than $15.00 per hour. Forty percent of Americans can't afford a $400 bill, whether it's medical or fixing their car. Fifteen per cent of the American population make minimum wage." Dimon also added that the education system is broken and sometimes a college education is worthless. I discuss the student loan crisis and how you can navigate these scary waters in Chapter Two of this book. Dimon also mentions that 70,000 have died because of opioid abuse. In Chapter Ten, DUI and other Legal Calamities, *Get WalletWise, The Workbook* focuses on the financial tragedy that drug abuse causes.

That interview took place in March 2019. Just think how many more people are in trouble since the COVID-19 pandemic. In November 2020, 26 million Americans said they did not have enough to eat.

There are genuine problems in the American economy; you cannot afford to be frivolous with your money.

You learn that attorneys, financial advisors, car sales people, landlords, bankers, employees, employers… fill in the blank… may not be looking out for your best interest. You will develop the skills to know whom to trust. This book is the first step for you to get on the right track of money management.

How to Use this Workbook.

1. First, come up with a clear and positive mindset to motivate you to read and practice with the workbook. Just like Stephen Covey said in Habit 2; "Begin with the End in Mind." Find your *why*! Is your *why* a less stressful life, less debt in your life, or a better future paid for by your investments? Whatever your *why* is, make it a good one! When you get discouraged, think of your *why*, then get your mindset back on track.

2. As you go through this workbook on your journey working through the financial lessons and exercises, a best practice would be to imagine the financially literate person you will be in one to two years. Imagine your happy future self, right now. What will be your wallet in the future? Imagine it!
    "Everything you can imagine is real." - Pablo Picasso

3. Understand that this transformational process will take time. It can take years to see the benefits of a well-made plan.

4. Commit to a specific time and place to study. To develop the skills to create the positive habits that you need takes discipline. This discipline begins with a commitment to the material. Keep your attitude in check. Your investment in this work may not always be easy. That's totally normal. Learn resilience to stay the course. With the right attitude, you will see a positive change.

5. Try to read and practice daily. Start with fifteen to twenty minutes/day. Step-by-step you can increase that to 1 hour/day. But as long as you're doing a little more than yesterday, you're getting closer to your financial freedom.

6. Download and print the worksheets from this link. Place them inside your workbook or put them in a handy file folder so you can find them quickly.

There is a price for everything

The following is an excerpt from the website https://www.thestreet.com/. This is what Allyson Whipple (adjunct assistant professor at Austin Community College) said:

"A few years ago, I got myself into a bad financial situation. Although my parents had worked hard to impress upon me the importance of financial responsibility, I was apparently hell-bent on making mistakes.

I spent most of my twenties being irresponsible with credit cards and was only making minimum payments on my student loans. Then, I took a chance on a new job that didn't pan out and temped irregular, low-paying gigs for almost two years. And then, my husband needed hand surgery, and I had to max out a high-interest credit card I'd almost paid off so we could afford it.

In part, because of the chronic financial strain, my marriage fell apart. I found steady work at that point, but wasn't making a lot. So now I had an outrageous amount of debt, plus a divorce, and had to find a new place to live. This was especially scary because I owed the city $3,000 in past-due utility bills and couldn't get utilities set up at my place until I paid that back.

"I found a roommate who had the utilities in his name, and I went through credit counseling. I also got a friend to help support me by making sure I checked my bank balance and budget every day. While I'm still in debt, I'm digging myself out from under the hole."

So, what's the lesson that we can learn from Allyson?

You have a choice. Either create positive money habits through spending wisely and saving for the future, or start finding a roommate so he/she could help you with the utilities in the future. You might find it harsh, but it's a reality that you may have to pay for your bad habits. I hope you choose wisely and embrace learning new skills and positive habits!

Chapter 1

Credit Card Debt

I love money. I love everything about it. I bought some pretty good stuff. Got me a $300 pair of socks. Got a fur sink. An electric dog polisher. A gasoline-powered turtleneck sweater. And, of course, I bought some dumb stuff, too.

–Steve Martin

Post-Pandemic update

With layoffs skyrocketing during the outbreak and lockdowns, Americans have been piling on more credit card debt: 47% now carry balances, up from 43% in March (2020), and nearly a quarter say they've taken on more card debt amid the coronavirus downturn, a CreditCards.com survey found.

In an interview with Warren Buffett by Yahoo! finance, turning to credit cards because of financial hardship is one thing, but Buffett says some people use them as "a piggy bank to be raided."

He recently told his company's shareholders about a friend who came into a windfall and asked for advice on what to do with it. She also had credit card debt — at 18% interest.

"If I owed any money at 18%, the first thing I'd do with any money I had would be to pay it off," Buffett said he told her. "You can't go through life borrowing money at those rates and be better off."

You should be careful with credit cards

Credit cards, by design, are financial products that exploit our human nature to be happier. Credit cards are very convenient and may help enable an instant-gratification mentality.

"Young people are threatened... by the evil use of advertising techniques that stimulate the natural inclination to avoid hard work by promising the immediate satisfaction of every desire." — Pope John Paul II

The more emotional a seller can get you through advertising a product or service, the more you will spend on impulse. When convinced a particular purchase will make us feel better, we will make the purchase. If a business can convince us that the purchase makes us "seem" successful, then we will buy more.

Businesses encourage us to use our credit cards for the purchase because we do not suffer the same psychological pain we do when we pay with cash. We are paying with a magic plastic card! We feel no pain for our purchase.

The greatest test to determine if you are overspending is carrying a balance on your credit card. Do you carry an unpaid balance on your credit card? You may be an over spender. If you are not an over spender, then pay off your credit card balances monthly and avoid the interest charges. If you don't pay off your balance each month, your credit card bank charges your account nosebleed interest rates, usually above 18%. The average credit card interest rate is 21% (at the time of printing). Besides the interest rate, banks charge you overpriced "over the credit line" fees and "late" fees. Another reason I wrote this book is to help you save money by avoiding these high fees.

Credit card solutions

I have created three different approaches to managing your credit card accounts depending upon your ability to pay the balance in full each month or if you are carrying a balance.

This is awkward:

Next, I ask you to ask yourself a few important questions. Please be honest with yourself.

Questions

Exercise Time: minimum 15 minutes.

❖ *How do you feel about credit?*

❖ *What exactly is responsible credit use? Are you responsible with credit?*

❖ *Do you make impulse purchases with your credit card?*

❖ *How many credit cards do you have?*

❖ *Do you pay your credit card balances in full on your card monthly?*

How did that go? Not too bad, right?

If you are in a classroom setting, ask the person on your left our right to share your answers.

Your next assignment is to map out your credit cards on the following Credit Card Debt List.

Download this easy-to-use form from: https://www.walletwise.org/creditcards

Credit Card Debt List

Creditor	Debt Amount	Monthly Payment	Interest Rate	Months Past Due
Credit Card # 1	$	$		
Credit Card # 2				
Credit Card # 3				
Credit Card # 4				
Credit Card # 5				
Credit Card # 6				
Total Credit Card Debt	$	$		

You can start the process by collecting your credit cards. Then print your statements from your online accounts. Locate the balance owed and put that under debt amount. Add the monthly payment you can afford. Find and list the interest rate. Are your accounts past due? This is an extremely important exercise. Please do not pass it by. We can use this information to decide if we will snowball or avalanche your debt, as discussed in Level 2 of the following credit card debt categories.

Let's discuss the 3 unique plans of action depending on your credit card debt situation.

Level one

If you hold an unpayable balance on your credit cards and are having difficulty with your personal finances, and you can never pay the balances in full each month, then cut the credit cards. That's right, get a pair of scissors and physically cut the cards in half and dispose of them. That's the price you pay for not being able to use a credit card. Can you fix this? Yes. You live by a four-letter word: CASH!

This is good news. Remember, I said above that people do not equate wallet-sized pieces of plastic with the pain and suffering they feel when spending cold, hard cash on a purchase. You will now do a better job determining if that next purchase is a want, a desire, or an absolute necessity.

Remember to sign up for alerts and automatic payment so you are never late again on your credit card payments and become liable to late fees.

"Wait a minute," you say. "Why do I need to do this? I just cut up my cards." Just because you cut up your card does not mean your accounts no longer exist. You still have the account. You cut up your cards to eliminate your ability to use them card to spend more. The accounts still exist, and you still owe the money.

If you possess the skill to negotiate, contact the credit card company and ask them for a lower interest rate. Tell them you are considering switching to a new credit card with a better interest rate. This only works if you are up to date on your payments.

Use the table below to manage with cash while your credit card accounts cool off.

Use this table as a "habit tracker"

Step No.	Description	Status
1	Determine which expenditures you can pay in cash!	
2	List categories like groceries, entertainment, eating out, and clothing	
3	To reduce your spending, only use cash for these categories	
4	Do not use debit cards, credit cards, nor check book	
5	Disconnect any automatic payments connected to your credit card	
6	Keep your debit card at home until you get a handle on your spending	
The Envelope Riddle	A simple way to keep track of your cash expenditures is to use the envelope system. Make an envelope for each budget item and put the correct amount of cash. When an envelope is empty, then you are done spending in that category. Put paid receipts into the correct envelope to see how much money you spent in that category.	

This new adventure will be difficult, but one worth taking. When I had overwhelming credit card debt, I used this method to get back on track. Was it easy? No. Was I tempted to break out another credit card? Yes. But, I didn't. You can do this. I have faith in you.

You should develop a procedure to manage your cash. Using cash may be inconvenient, but it is a great way to get a handle on your spending and reduce impulsive credit card usage.

Please see the following article to unpack this idea.

https://www.thebalance.com/how-to-switch-to-cash-only-for-your-budget-2385691

In Chapter Four, "Money Management and Your Budget," I will discuss how to run a ledger to keep track of your cash, which is an alternative to the envelope method.

Warning:

You should not do business with a debt relief, debt settlement, or debt consolidation company.

How to function without a credit card:

Despite what many people say, you can function in life very well without a credit card. You should get a pre-paid debit card. The pre-paid debit card limits your liability. It's not cash, and many pre-paid card companies include fraud protection. If you travel, there are rental car companies and hotels that have payment alternatives to cash.

Start by getting a prepaid debit card. One of my favorites is PayPal Prepaid Mastercard https://www.paypal-prepaid.com/. I suggest opening a PayPal account. No PayPal account? You can try MOVO prepaid debit card. https://movo.cash/

NerdWallet, the Balance, Credit Karma, the Simple Dollar, and Money Under 30 recommend MOVO as one of the best prepaid debit cards. There is no credit check, and you can make quick direct deposits, according to their website. I do not recommend that you set up direct deposit money into this account as a replacement for your checking account. Instead, you can transfer money from your checking account to this prepaid card for planned incidental expenses. Your money is safer because you only risk the money in the prepaid account and do not risk the money in your checking account.

"But Ken, I need a credit card to rent a car." Not true!

https://www.daveramsey.com/blog/rent-a-car-without-a-credit-card

You should check out Dollar rental car. They will rent a car with a non-prepaid debit card.

"But Ken, I need a credit card to book a hotel room." Not true! Hotels will take reservations and process payment through a debit card. They will put a hold on it as a deposit for one or two nights, depending on the hotel. So, it's an excellent idea to deposit money in your account before you travel.

Remember to sign up for alerts and automatic payment so you are never late again on your credit card payment.

Level two

If you are using credit cards and hold balances on your credit card, remove the credit cards from your wallet and put them into a sealable sandwich bag, pour water into the bag, and place them in your freezer. Put those cards on ice!!

Literally!

This removes the opportunity for impulse purchases. Transfer your card balance to a lower interest card while you repay this card balance. There are credit cards specifically designed with this idea in mind. I suggest contacting your local credit union for the best interest rate and professional banking services.

Pay off the credit card balance faster by paying the minimum payment, divide the payment in half, then pay your credit card payment every two weeks. You want the power of compounding to benefit you. By paying more often, you receive the reward of less overall interest being charged against you. Don't pay one payment of $200 every month, instead, pay $100 every 14 days.

By doing so, you can pay off your debt balance 75% faster. You weren't expecting this, right? Yes, you can pay your debts way faster by following this method rather than paying just the minimum payment. Also, keep your payment (14 days) the same. Do your best to pay more than the minimum payment. Whatever that monthly budgeted amount is, divide in half and pay every two weeks to get compounding to benefit you.

Another key aspect is to keep your payment the same. Just because you are making progress and the credit card says, "Now you can pay less," doesn't mean you should do so. Don't reduce your payment. You will never get ahead.

The credit card statement below will tell you how long it will take for you to pay off the balance if you just pay the minimum payment. The statement will also show you the inflated amount of interest you will pay.

Late Payment Warning: If we do not receive your minimum payment by the date listed above, you may have to pay a late fee of up to $40 and your APRs may be increased up to the Penalty APR of 29.99%.

Minimum Payment Warning: If you make only the minimum payment each period, you will pay more in interest and it will take you longer to pay off your balance. For example:

If you make no additional charges using this card and each month you pay...	You will pay off the balance shown on the statement in about...	And you will end up paying an estimated total of...
Only the minimum payment	17 year(s)	$9,194
$175	3 year(s)	$6,300 (Savings = $2,894)

For information about credit counseling services, call 1-877-337-8187.

If you only pay the minimum payment, you will pay $9,194 over 17 years. The credit card company reports an arbitrary amount of $175. If you pay $175, then you save almost $2,900 in interest fees.

To check how much interest you can save by paying off your balance faster, check out the following link:

https://www.bankrate.com/finance/credit-cards/credit-card-payoff-calculator/

Snowballs and Avalanches Debt Payoff Strategies

Financial gurus developed these concepts as debt reduction strategies to help debtors better understand how their debt is getting lower. In addition, some people prefer one method over the other because of their perceived speed their debt is being repaid. This can make it easier to see that you are making progress and your hard work is paying off.

Check out this amazing site to help you get a handle on runaway debt.

The following notice is from their website:

"Undebt.it is a debt payment manager that will generate a plan for you to get out of debt by paying extra amounts on certain accounts until you pay them off. All the <u>payment plans</u> that Undebt.it can use are all **rollover** plans, meaning that they roll extra payments from one debt to the next and so on. Dave Ramsey encourages this type of debt payment system. Dave Ramsey's Debt Snowball generically popularized it. The two most popular payment plans are the debt snowball (paying the lowest balance account first) and the debt avalanche (paying the account with the highest interest rate first) which is also called 'debt stacking.' You can use either of those plans with Undebt.it or one of the several other methods detailed below. The debt avalanche is mathematically the most effective, but all the rollover methods work well and will get you debt free in a similar amount of time; just choose the plan which works the best for your situation. Remember, you can change the payment plan."

Debt Snowball	Debt Avalanche
Paying the lowest balance account first	Paying the account with the highest interest rate first
Gives you a faster sense of accomplishment as you will get rid of debt from your accounts faster	It makes sense because the longer you hold a debt at a higher interest rate, the more interest will accumulate
The best approach is to move on to the next smallest debt once you have paid off the smallest debt on another of your accounts	The best approach is to pay the minimum amount on the remaining debt accounts and pay as much as you can on the highest interest rate account first
Another advantage to this method is that it lowers the number of outstanding accounts, allowing you to build more focus with your payments	Once you have completed paying the debt for highest interest rate account, move on to the next highest interest rate account
Repeat the process until your debt free	Repeat the process until your debt free

Debt Snowball Calculator and Debt Reduction Assistant

Try https://undebt.it/, free online, mobile-friendly application that creates an easy-to-follow payment plan.

The "Snowball and Avalanche" debt repayment methods are the favorite methods of reducing debt repayment. The avalanche method uses extra money to pay off your high interest rate debts first. This makes sense because the longer you hold a debt at a higher interest rate, the more interest will accumulate. Pay the minimum payment on the remaining debt accounts and focus on paying as much as you can afford on the highest interest rate account first. Once you complete paying off the highest interest rate account, move to the next highest interest rate account. Repeat this process until you are debt free.

The snowball method pays off the smallest debt balance first, giving you a faster sense of accomplishment. Once you pay off the smallest debt, move on to the next smallest debt etc…Another advantage of this method is the fact that you will lower the number of accounts you have with outstanding balances.

How to Pay Down Debt

When you carry a balance on your credit cards, there are a few additional words of wisdom that can help you pay down the balance faster. You should transfer the balance to a low interest credit card. My suggestion is to start a relationship with your local credit union. They have great rates and a no-nonsense approach to credit card customer service. For example, I just went to my credit union website and they have a balance transfer card at 1.9% for 15 months, no balance transfer fee (that's good) and no annual fee (that's golden!).

You could get a debt consolidation/personal loan from your credit union or bank. Another benefit is the fact that a personal loan is a fixed interest payment that results in a fixed monthly payment.

Here is the problem: Many of my financial coaching clients went to their banker and qualified for a debt consolidation/personal loan to pay off their credit card debt. The problem is that my clients never got a handle on their budget or excessive spending habits. They continued to use their credit card irresponsibly, racking up additional debt after agreeing to refinance their old credit card debt with a debt consolidation/personal loan. Now, they have "double trouble!" They have a balance on their card... again! They also now have a regular monthly payment on their debt consolidation/personal note. That is why I strongly suggest you take your credit cards and put them in a freezer bag and throw them in the freezer. Get another trustworthy person to hold you accountable to stop using your credit cards until you pay the debt consolidation loan off.

Pay off on the loan may take three to five years. Then use the credit cards to purchase items you can only afford to repay monthly.

Let's discuss Level 3 and then I will show you some real-life experiences and what valuable lessons I have learned from them.

Level 3

If you use credit cards responsibly, carry only two credit cards on your person. One would come in handy as a backup and I will explain. Why only two? What if your wallet or purse gets stolen? More credit cards in your wallet open you up to a potentially larger fraud coverage ($50.00 per card) if the card is lost or stolen and then used to pay for a purchase. If you have over two credit cards, store the extra cards in a secure location like a safe or fireproof lockable file box. If someone steals your two cards, you have back up to your backup. You really should have backup payment cards in case of online or physical theft.

Never use a store credit card.

When you pay the balance of your card, every month, choose a card with no annual fee and a long grace period so you can make your payment before interest charges accrue.

The double backup:

Carry a debit card but try not to use it for gasoline purchases, hotel rooms, or rental cars, because they put holds that blocks access to your money in the checking account. If you scheduled an automatic auto or mortgage payment, you could trigger an insufficient fund episode. In addition, banks handle debit card fraud issues differently than credit card fraud. If you don't report or discover debit card fraud at once, you will be liable for $50.00 of the fraud (MOST high-tier credit cards charge 0) if you report within 48 hours. Between 48 hours and 60 days you are on the hook for up to $500, and after 60 days you are on the hook for the WHOLE amount.

Additional information

Credit card use opens you up to a variety of suboptimal events. Although not exclusive to credit cards, be aware of the possibility of identity theft and identity fraud that stem from the use of credit cards and credit accounts. This is another reason it is important for you to read your credit card statement at least monthly.

a) **Identity Theft:** This involves the theft of your personal financial and identification information online or offline.

b) **Identity Fraud:** Your stolen identity is used to withdraw cash, incur unauthorized charges, or open false accounts.

The Solutions
In order to create a system to protect your personal information, shred documents that contain personal information. You should buy a good shredder at Amazon.com.
To guard your passwords, try using 1Password, Dashlane or Sticky Passwords (these are excellent password managers).
Buy a lockable security box and store a paper copy of your passwords and important PINs.
Don't forget to limit the amount of personal information you display on social media applications like Facebook, Instagram, and Twitter.
As an additional safeguard, keep antivirus software on your computers and consider purchasing a VPN to protect you from the bad guys.

You must review your credit card and billing statements monthly. Balance your checkbook and sign up for e-mail and text alerts. This way, your accounts alert you when there is any legit or illegal activity.

Thieves can open accounts online with your birthdate and social security number. So, please guard your numbers!

Managing Your Credit Card Account

The following Credit Card Rules conversation will help you understand how to manage your credit card and understand our responsibilities when using a credit card. This section will discuss how to read our credit card statement, collect our bonus points, manage and cancel "gray" charges, handle credit card disputes, and more.

Did you know that Credit Card application is a contract?

Every credit card has an agreement (a friendly word for contract). I suggest you become familiar with the important items in that agreement. Credit card agreements have price information. The pricing section includes the introductory interest they charge you, separated by purchases and credit card transfers. The statement displays the APR (annual percentage rate) for cash advances. They display the grace period time between the end of the billing cycle and the beginning of interest charges. Here is an example of a Capital One's Pricing Information.

:

CAPITAL ONE PRICING INFORMATION	
Annual Percentage Rate (APR) for Purchases	Introductory rate of 0% to 9.99%, ranging from 9 months to 18 months. Non-introductory rates between 14.24% and 28.24%. Some Purchase APRs may vary with the market based on changes in the Prime Rate.
APR for Transfers	Introductory rate of 0% to 9.99%, ranging from 9 months to 18 months. Non-introductory rates between 14.24% and 28.24%. Some Transfer APRs may vary with the market based on changes in the Prime Rate.
APR for Cash Advances	Non-introductory rates between 23.74% and 28.24%. Cash Advance APRs may vary with the market based on changes in the Prime Rate.
Paying Interest	Your due date is at least 25 days after the close of each billing cycle. We will not charge you interest on new purchases, provided you have paid your previous balance in full by the due date each month. We will begin charging interest on cash advances and transfers on the transaction date.
Minimum Interest Charge	If you are charged interest, the charge will be no less than $0.50.
Annual Fee	Between $0 and $39 annually.
Transaction Fees	
• Transfer Fee • Cash Advance Fee	3% of the amount of each transfer. The greater of either $10 or 3% of the amount of each cash advance.
Penalty Fees	
• Late Payment	Up to $38.

This is only the first part of Capital One's credit card agreement. The second part is the Customer Agreement. This part includes all the provisos, limitations, and addendum. Credit lines and credit limits are the most important parts of the Customer Agreement. The bank establishes these rules. The Authorized User section describes the rules involving the additional "persons" you have allowed to use your card. Remember that you are financially responsible for anything your "authorized" user does with your account. I would suggest you do not allow "authorized" users on your account. Have other persons get their own accounts. If they cannot qualify for an account, have them get their own debit card like Greenlight debit card, www.greenlightcard.com. This section also discusses the handling of disputes and a list of fees such as Stop Payment Fees on access checks, cash advance fees, transfer fees, membership fees, late payment fee, and returned payment fees.

Do you see a pattern? A lot of money in the form of fees leaves your wallet and ends up in the credit card company's wallet. Credit card companies charge high fees for late payments and over the credit limit problems. Please avoid them. If you don't read your credit card statement, these fees get tacked on without your knowledge. Ignorance of the terms of your contract is not a good plan or defense.

Look at the $38.00 late payment fee you pay in the above statement! Sorry, but that is how it works. If you want the so-called "privilege" of using a credit card, then read and understand the contract. I suggest you read the fine print of the agreements before you sign. The contract favors the credit card company and not you!

You have legal rights! The Fair Credit Billing Act protects you against debt collection harassment and abuse, credit bureau abuse, and discrimination. You should see www.ftc.gov and search for the Fair Credit Billing Act.

Instead, establish an emergency fund

Instead of using your credit card as a piggy bank to pay for emergencies and unexpected expenses, set up an emergency fund to pay for emergencies. See Chapter Four, "Money Management and Your Budget."

You should be proactive with your credit card management. One of my financial coach clients shared a story where he called credit card customer service to dispute the reversal of a Sun Pass charge that was legitimate but flagged as a fraud. That's Florida's toll road payment system. He found out when he attempted to pay for gas with the card. The gas station denied the card for payment. He received no e-mails or texts. No phone call that there was a problem. A denied purchase was the first feedback they received. He went to check the account online and

He could not access the account. No reason was given. He called the 1-800 number on the website and got an automated response. When he finally got through to customer service, he found the charges in question were two weeks old.

None of the charges were fraudulent.

Result: Card canceled. New one will arrive in the mail.

Take Away: Please make sure you have a backup plan in case they decline your credit card.

The easiest way to use a credit card is to only purchase items you can afford to pay for by the end of the credit card's billing cycle. This allows you to use the card's purchasing power without paying interest to the bank. If you are currently carrying a balance on your credit card account, fear not; we will discuss what we can do to fix that problem.

In addition, you must be careful about credit card charge errors.

Just as important as reading the credit card agreement is to read your credit card statement at least monthly. It may be wiser to look at the statement weekly until you have established a legitimate system of managing and monitoring your accounts.

By reading my credit card statements regularly, I found: If ignored, the vendor would happily charge my credit card and receive my money for nothing.

    a.   I opened my Discover statement. This account has a small balance left over from a zero-interest balance transfer I made about 2 years ago. I paid the difference between the statement balance and the payoff balance. I noticed that now I have an interest charge on the statement. That's right, the balance transfer offer expired. Hmm. Let's check the interest rate. 21%. Really? Paying that off as soon as possible.

b. *Post COVID-19 note: At the end of January 2020, Discover sent me a letter that my account was closed for non-use. Our takeaway is that you should charge something small on a zero balance card to keep it active. I lost that credit line. Not a huge deal, but closed credit accounts can cause your FICO credit score to go down due to you using a higher credit utilization ratio.*

c. I received a text alert (Ask Trim) from Citi card. $19.99 charged by an app via Apple iCloud. I started a free financial application expecting the FREE app trial to go away as they did not have my credit card number because I did not update my credit card on iCloud. Right, I shut myself off from the app store. Nope, Apple got the new number. Four weeks after the FREE trial ended, the app charged my card to reactivate. I went online and disputed the charge, and they removed it.

My point here is that credit cards are a powerful financial tool that you must manage carefully by monitoring statements monthly.

Please, we must read every credit card statement at least monthly.

You must reach out to credit card customer service every time there is an issue, no matter how large or small! You must check your account statement and activity online every month!

Here's an example of what one of my credit card statements looks like. This is a credit card I got through a relationship with AAA. The credit card company is called ACG Services. This part of the statement is the Summary.

New Balance	$102.84
Minimum Payment Due	$30.00
Payment Due Date	08/01/2019

Late Payment Warning: If we do not receive your minimum payment by the date listed above, you may have to pay up to a $39.00 Late Fee.

AAA Dollars Gas Rebate Summary

| Earned this Statement | $2.06 |
| Earned Year to Date | $30.74 |

For details, see your rebate section.

Activity Summary

Previous Balance	+	$166.14
Payments	-	$162.82CR
Other Credits	-	$3.32CR
Purchases	+	$102.84
Balance Transfers		$0.00
Advances		$0.00
Other Debits		$0.00
Fees Charged		$0.00
Interest Charged		$0.00
New Balance	=	**$102.84**
Past Due		**$0.00**
Minimum Payment Due		**$30.00**
Revolving Line of Credit		$24,900.00
Revolving Line Available		$24,797.16
Days in Billing Period		29

All credit cards are 0% interest if you don't carry a balance!

What this means may not be obvious to everyone at first glance. Credit cards only charge interest when you carry a balance. If you pay the balance of the card each month, you pay zero in interest. This means you pay nothing for the purchasing power created by the credit card.

However, it is still possible to pay your outstanding balance monthly, but the credit card charges you an annual fee. It's like the price you pay for the credit card company to be friends with you. Don't fall for this. Get a credit card sponsored by your credit union with low or no annual fee.

Please pay your balance in full each month.

This part of the statement is the detail of the transactions.

Transactions

Payments and Other Credits

Post Date	Trans Date	Ref #	Transaction Description	Amount
06/05			AAA STATEMENT CREDIT CREDIT ADJUSTMENT	$3.32CR
07/01	07/01	MTC	PAYMENT THANK YOU	$162.82CR
			TOTAL THIS PERIOD	**$166.14CR**

Purchases and Other Debits

Post Date	Trans Date	Ref #	Transaction Description	Amount
06/12	06/10	8827	SHELL OIL 12589641005 JACKSONVILLE FL	$26.28
06/24	06/20	1720	RACETRAC 196 00001966 ORANGE PARK FL	$24.76
06/26	06/24	3632	QT 1715 97017156 KENNESAW GA	$36.55
06/27	06/26	0373	SQ *SQ *GLOVER PARK BR MARIETTA GA	$15.25
			TOTAL THIS PERIOD	**$102.84**

2019 Totals Year-to-Date	
Total Fees Charged in 2019	$0.00
Total Interest Charged in 2019	$0.00

Please note the highlighted 2019 Total Fees and Total Interest Charges.

They are 0.00. Zero is your goal! Please note the AAA credit statement credit adjustment noted above. This card with AGC Card Services (partnered with AAA) automatically credits back your points for purchasing gas with the AAA card. More on this later in this chapter, but I use this card for only paying for gas. It doubles as my backup card in case my major card is not working.

Side Bar: AAA

AAA is an amazing personal finance resource. AAA is an insurance company and bank besides being an automobile club. AAA sells auto, boat, RV, life, renters, flood and home insurance. AAA is a bank. Not only do they partner with banks that issue credit cards, but they also have access to savings and checking accounts, mortgages and reputable personal loans. They also have an auto buying service. I will mention AAA in Chapter Ten, "DUI and other Legal Calamities." AAA is a leader in teaching the public about the ills associated with distracted driving, aggressive driving, as well as drinking and driving.

The next statement is from the card I do the bulk of my bill paying with. I paid a little interest in 2019. Did you notice the cash advance interest rate mentioned in the statement? Cash advances are 27.49%. Boo! The reason I mention the Cash Advance rate here is to let you know how expensive it is to borrow cash from your credit card account. We should not use credit cards as an ATM. Banks created credit cards to assist us in buying consumer goods. Credit card companies collect fees from you as interest in carrying balances and store merchant fees. When you borrow cash from your credit card, you pay a higher interest rate because the credit card company considers you the borrower and the merchant. Please don't borrow cash from your credit card account unless it is an absolute emergency! You should equally repay the amount as soon as possible.

Interest charged

Total interest charged in this billing period	$0.00

2019 totals year-to-date

Total fees charged in 2019	$0.00
Total interest charged in 2019	$107.14

Interest charge calculation

Days in billing cycle: **33**

Your **Annual Percentage Rate (APR)** is the annual interest rate on your account.

Balance type	Annual percentage rate (APR)	Balance subject to interest rate	Interest charge
PURCHASES			
Standard Purch	12.24% (V)	$0.00 (D)	$0.00
ADVANCES			
Standard Adv	27.49% (V)	$0.00 (D)	$0.00

Credit Card Bonus Points: Do not forget to redeem your bonus points. You should apply bonus points to your balance instead of buying something with them on impulse. I've worked with multiple clients who forgot this credit card reward and when discovered, they reduced their balance owed!

Log on to your credit card's website and locate the procedure for redeeming points.

Do Read your statement to discover if your credit card is changing its billing, interest, or "details" about your account. Credit card companies often change the rules of the game in the middle of the game. In addition, if you see unacceptable terms, I suggest you transfer to a new card. If you have bad credit, you won't be able to apply for a new, better card.

ThankYou Points Earned This Period	
2x on Dining	497
2x on Entertainment	0
1x on Other Purchases	2,390
Total Earned	**2,887**

» Visit
to redeem points or see
full rewards details.

Bonus Points may take one to two billing cycles to appear on your statement. Please refer to the specific terms and conditions pertaining to the promotion for further details.

Important Changes to Your Account Terms

The following is a summary of changes being made to your account terms. Your Citi Flex Plan APR is changing to align with your APR for Purchases. These changes will take effect on September 02, 2019. For more information, please see **"Details About the Changes"** below.

The current *Interest Rates and Interest Charges* section of the Fact Sheet (Pricing Information Table) will be revised as follows:

Revised Terms as of September 02, 2019	
APR for Citi Flex Plan	**12.24%** This APR will vary with the market based on the Prime Rate.

The current Details About *Your Interest Rates and Interest Calculations* section of the Fact Sheet (Pricing Information Table) will be revised as follows:

Details About Your Interest Rates and Interest Calculations	Periodic Rate as of 06/24/2019	For variable rates: U.S. Prime Rate Plus
Citi Flex Plan APR	0.03353% (D)	6.74%

Do you want to have a credit card? Remember, The Golden Rule says, "Those that have the Gold make the Rules". If you don't like the rules, then it's not mandatory that you must have a credit card. Please understand that credit cards are real debt contracts.

Beware of Gray charges. These are repetitive charges to your card that never go away even after you cancel them, such as your magazine, free trial, or software subscriptions, among others. You can fight this abuse by checking your credit card statement at least monthly. Many credit cards allow you to dispute charges online by simply following the credit card dispute process. If you carry a zero balance, cancel any credit card that continues to bill you for disputed charges. Don't do business with a credit card company that does not play fair. CITI card allows you to file the dispute online with no hassle. You can also contact the vendor. You should cancel that unused, unwanted, and unneeded magazine and online video streaming subscription, or similar liabilities, now. However, consumer aware, the vendor may turn on their heavy sales pitch to convince you to keep whatever service they are selling.

I'm a bad boy! Another way to remove gray charges is to ask your credit card company to issue a new card as if you were reporting your credit card as lost or stolen. Have your card replaced with a new card that comes with a new card number. This will automatically make the gray charges disappear. Remember, though, to update any account that you want to keep. This can help you discover unnecessary charges lurking in the background.

Updated Development I have noticed are that subscriptions transfer from the expired card to the new card without your permission. I told you credit card companies can be sneaky!

Children with credit cards to access online video games

There are many stories on the internet sharing the traps developed by the gaming industry. It is a free country. Adults are free to max out their credit card dressing their character in a video game. But what if I tell you that children under 18 playing video games allowed by their parents and then rack up thousands of dollars in credit card bills by purchasing additional "In-app" purchases? "Gaming is a World of Heavy Sales Pressure and Frictionless Theft," says Evan V. Simon.

Parents discovered the charges of their children, which resulted in financial hardship for years. There are no safeguards with online gaming; no cashier to stop reckless spending. Worse still, there is no tangible product to return to the store for a refund.

Online gaming addiction is a problem. Free mobile games make most of their money from "In-app" purchases from compulsive customers, says Simon.

In *Fortnite*, you can buy virtual clothes to upscale your character. You can play the game free forever, but if you want "bling" you can buy a Battle Pass or Battle Bundle. Kids racked over $4,000 in charges without realizing it and created a credit card statement with pages filled with many one and five dollar charges.

Credit Card Disputes

Credit cards have protections for its customers. If you received a good or service not as promised and the vendor does not want to remedy the situation, contact your credit card company and dispute the charge. They may send you an application to fill out to explain the product or service you purchased and the nature of your dissatisfaction. Many credit card companies will give you an immediate credit for your dispute until they resolve the dispute. The vendor tells their side of the story so the process can take 30-45 days. If the credit card company agrees with you, the temporary credit becomes permanent. The attached letter is an example of a credit card dispute regarding an auto repair that went badly. You should respond clearly, accurately, and proactively when mistreated by a vendor. In the situation mentioned here, my client was told to "pound sand" by the dealership service manager. Here, an independent auto mechanic verified my client's findings. The result is that the bank refunded the charges and another letter to the Subaru Corporation resulted in a cash settlement.

Credit Card Dispute Letter March 17, 2008

RE: ▮▮▮▮▮▮▮▮▮▮

As per customer agent discussion on March 12, 2008:
Please find a complete explanation of disputed charge.

Brought car to ▮▮▮▮▮▮▮▮▮▮ to repair oil leak. As indicated on repair estimate, I indicated an oil leak coming from the **back** of the engine. The service writer, Daniel, asked if I had performed very specific scheduled services. I said, no, I am here to fix the **oil leak** first. The service writer, before seeing the car intimated that neglecting to perform a timing chain replacement, along with certain oil seals, and replacing the water pump would stop the leak. These are all items at the **front** of the engine! After the mechanic Cliff, inspected the car, he diagnosed that the valve cover gaskets were leaking and that was the cause of the oil draining down the back of the engine. The mechanic stated that repairing the valve cover gaskets; along with scheduled maintenance service totaling over $1,200 would repair the problem. I considered them the experts and approved the repairs. (Please review the repair estimate. I do not have a copy that I signed authorizing a repair of the vehicle. This maybe the deal breaker right here!) 3 and one half weeks later I still had the same symptoms. I waited to see if the burnt oil smell would disappear after repairs were done. They did not. On 1/21/07 (see attached report) another mechanic verified that original problem not repaired. He discovered a leaking head gasket that had been leaking for some time. See attached 2nd opinion of mechanic indicating these initial repairs were irrelevant for the leaking head gasket. I was billed $1,200 for irrelevant repairs and to had to return the car to the dealer to repair what should have been diagnosed and repaired correctly the first time. I am paying for their mistake. In fact, I found a website www.subaruheadgasket.com that indicates that this is a very common problem with my year and model of Subaru and described symptoms exactly as mine. It would seem the experts would be aware of this problem. In fact the service manager, Rene told me, "They have been repairing a lot of these." So why was it so difficult to properly diagnose my problem in the first place?.....the experts did not find it. That's the problem. In addition when I went back the second time to Palm Chrysler Subaru to repair the head gasket, Subaru corporation participated in paying for one half (admitting design flaw) of the head gasket repair. If the diagnosis had been correct in the first place, would have Subaru Corporation helped in the overall repair? We will never know. I got stuck with the bill.

In addition, the engine overhaul was done hastily. After one week I discovered the air conditioning inoperative and a few days later, the car stalled completely with a code for a defective crank sensor. I had the car towed back to the dealership at my expense for warranty repair. I left the auto with them a week to make certain it was repaired properly. The entire time, there was no admission of wrongdoing and the statement preceded every explanation, "We will have to check to verify what your saying is true." Every time! They admitted nothing and I received no apology for their negligence!

The reason I did not report this sooner as I thought disputing the charge would jeopardize a competent repair job. They would have also refused to refund my towing bill. I also risked losing the car to the shop if the dealership considered my dispute a reason of non-payment. I could not risk either circumstance. Yes, believe it or not, a repair estimate starting on Dec. 26, 2007 was not officially completed until I received the towing reimbursement on March 12, 2007. (Please see attached check stub.)

My goal is to have the disputed charges refunded to my account. I spoke with the general manager, Troy, on March 13, 2007, and he told me to get lost! The repairs of 12-26-2007 were irrelevant to the leaking head gasket that a second mechanic had to locate. His second opinion response agrees that the Dec. 26, 2007 repairs were irrelevant and says so on his letterhead. I have done everything AAA credit card has asked to resolve this situation.

In Conclusion

Credit cards are powerful. When used responsibly with planning and discipline, they can make your financial life very convenient. In addition, responsible use of credit cards allows you to pay for goods and services regardless of your account balance. You should locate and visit your local credit union. Relative to other financial institutions, credit unions look out for your best interest.

Chapter 1

Credit card Debt

Summary Questions

Please answer these questions. Revisit your answers later, after you've started implementing the lessons in this chapter, to see if you feel differently about credit card debt. I am confident that you will notice a significant difference in perception of your spending habits.

I. *Do you carry an unpaid balance on your credit card?*

II. *Why do you think it is important to sign up for alerts and automatic payments?*

III. *Let's suppose you have lost your wallet/purse with your credit cards in it. What's the best way to avoid this kind of scenario?*

IV. *How do credit card fees affect your finances?*

V. *What laws protect you from credit card company misbehavior? Imagine a scenario where you have to protect your own rights and write a response letter.*

VI.   *What is the Consumer Financial Protection Bureau?*

VII.   *Which of the methods would you choose? Debt Snowball or Debt Avalanche? State your reasons and, if possible, devise a plan that you think will work out for this.*

VIII.   *What are Gray charges and what's the best way to avoid them?*

A short task!

A.   *On a sheet of paper, write all the likely areas where you can reduce your credit card spending. Compare these insights with your worksheets. Next (in your mind) think of the best action plan that will help you adopt these improved habits permanently (nothing complex, just keep it simple). Once you have a plan in mind, write it down and display your plan somewhere in your personal space so you can see it daily.*

B.   *Go online and surf the website https://www.consumerfinance.gov/. Find the Credit Card Agreement Database. There is a dropdown that allows you to find any major bank credit card agreement. Find the agreements associated with your personal credit cards. Download the PDF on your computer or print it if that is convenient.*

Chapter 2

Student Loans

"Education is the way out of the poverty trap. It shouldn't be the poverty trap itself and make those trying to better themselves incur massive student debt."

— Stewart Stafford

Ahh, the thrill of attending college. It reminds me of the board game *Life. The Game of Life* gave you the chance to attend college and borrow student loan debt you repaid later, after you started earning big bucks. In the board game, you ended up with a higher paying job that offset the increased debt load you possessed compared to the player who went straight to work. By the end of the game, the college graduates usually finished the *Game of Life* with the most assets. Oh my, have times changed?!

Note to Reader: I discuss alternatives to student loans later in this chapter

College education costs, which includes tuition, room and board and supplies, have skyrocketed. Student loan amounts have ballooned to keep up with college costs. Students who receive large financial aid packages in the form of scholarships still have to borrow enormous amounts of money to pay the bills. We leave these important decisions to 19 to 25-year-old students that have (according to the same intellectuals running the colleges) maturing brains. A friend of mine responded to this statement by asking, "For those first entering college, wouldn't you say a lot of those decisions are made together with parents? They're often the ones filling out financial aid paperwork, etc.?" My response is, "No. The admission counselors deliberately whisk students away from the parents at orientation to be sold classes the students may or may not need." This happened to my daughter. Survive this process by having an amazing relationship with your children and having a big conversation with your students before they enter the college admissions office by themselves. Independent adult creation is the goal. Parental supervision is no longer required. We think the advisor is our friend and expert when, in fact, the adviser is protecting the interests of the college. Your student may be inexperienced at this level of negotiations. I believe in teenagers becoming independent adults who learn by making mistakes. The college is negotiating with your student, with which AP, IB, and AICE classes they will accept. It benefits the college to accept none of them so that the college can sell your child more classes. This is one reason it takes six years for your student to complete a four-year program. My daughter, upon entering the University of South Florida, went to the admissions office without us and bought a class of German even though she was a Francophile. She had taken French classes throughout high school. Why not be consistent with her past classes and take French? No, German. Well, it helped her sing the German pieces in the chorus. This story is humorous now, and not a big deal. Be careful, for it could be much more serious. A friend of my daughter, in a public Florida university, was in the engineering program. One semester before he was ready to graduate, the university changed the graduation requirements of the degree. I suspect the university had an unpaid bill to pay and needed to raise extra revenue. My daughter's friend ended up enrolling for an added semester of courses to complete his degree. He had no other choice but to pay the tuition for another semester. As I have mentioned in other sections of this book, bankers, lawyers, real estate agents, and even college admission agents are not looking out for your best interest. They work under competing agendas. Caveat emptor! That is Latin for "Buyer beware!"

A recent Wall Street article reports that most college freshmen do not have the emotional maturity to make complex financial and life decisions alone. So, what could go wrong? Plenty! College financing is more complicated than shopping for a mortgage. In college, they redo the finance paperwork every year!

Data analyzed from the Federal Reserve's 2018 survey on the Economic Well-Being of U.S. Households reports over half of young adults who attended college borrowed to pay for their education. Most borrowers stay current on their payments. Many borrowers paid their loans. However, twenty percent of debtors (those who owe money) are behind on their payments. Private college students and individuals who did not finish their degree program fare worse. These issues are why I wrote this workbook for you.

Fun Student Loan Facts

- According to oneclass.com, fifty-seven percent of students that take on student loans don't graduate! And yes, the default rate of dropouts is higher than the default rate for graduates.

- Most students financed their degrees with student loans. Other forms of debt included credit cards and home equity loans. Debt in 2018 ranged from $20,000 to $25,000. Combining federal and private debt, the debt level equates to $30,000 per student.

- Among those making payments on their student loans, the typical median monthly payment is between $200 and $299 per month. The average payment per month is $393. (this statistic is skewed because of expensive medicine and law degrees)

- First generation college students are more likely to be late in their payments. First generation borrowers under thirty years of age are twice as likely to be behind on their payments.

I've read many newspaper articles, online news pieces, and blogs describing the experience of going to college, searching for, and finding a desirable field of study, only to end up with a college degree that is useless (unmarketable), and a student saddled with $50,000, $60,000, even $90,000 in debt.

The graduate struggles to make loan payments while driving a $500 car and living at home while working at a minimum wage job. Where did the money go? To the ivory tower. Colleges should be ashamed at what they are doing. JP Morgan chairperson and CEO Jamie Dimon called student lending in the U.S. a "disgrace" and said, "It's hurting America". They are setting up students for failure. The "Federal Student Loan Programs" factsheet gives sage advice under the "How Much Should I Borrow?" paragraph. The fact sheet says to research your future career at https://www.ls.gov/ooh/ and find your salary. Then the fact sheet says your student loan payments should be a small percentage of your salary after you graduate. That completes the depth of the financial advice given by the FSA (Federal Student Aid) about "student borrowing" common sense. There is no discussion of the possibility of changing your mind and then changing your major after you start college. Colleges love students who change majors. Back to the drawing board. Those physics "classes" now don't apply to your declared biology major. The students pay for the new classes and take out more student loans. This adds to the cost of an overpriced rite of passage. Thirty percent of college students change their majors at least once. Ten percent of students change over two times. Fifty-two percent of students majoring in mathematics change their majors. The statistics for college graduation rates show that only 28% of students finish their four-year degree within four years. In fact, the government measures the statistic for graduation rates in terms of students completing a four-year program within **six** years. Why does it take students six years to complete a four-year program? At public two-year colleges, 26% of students take three years to complete a two-year degree! SAT/ACT exam scores determine the success rate of students completing college. Why don't colleges have students take a battery of emotional, skills-based, and talent-based tests to better predict student success in completing college and finding a rewarding careers? This may reduce college major change and college dropout rates. (at the cost of lower revenues at colleges)

College Industrial Complex

College is not for everyone. High schools crank out diplomas and encourage (push) students to go to college. Colleges recruit large numbers of academically unqualified students, not up to the challenge, to pay for their "amazing," amenity-filled campuses. Do you see the irony? We, the college elite, want to produce an independent young adult. Our campus has the finest luxury dormitories, so your child will be "middle class" comfortable, though he or she could succeed with the basics. Your student borrows more to pay for unnecessary amenities that attract students to the college. The colleges charge higher tuition to pay for better amenities, and the cycle continues. Universities spare no expense.

The total number of U.S. student loan borrowers exceed 42.3 million. That's over 12.5% of the U.S. population! Students and graduates between eighteen and twenty-nine have most of the student loan debt. They owe about $1 trillion out of $1.67 trillion total. Student loan debt is the second highest national debt category after home mortgages.

College Board estimates the average annual in-state cost for tuition, room and board, fees, books and supplies at a four-year university is $21,370. That's real money.

According to Pew Research, one-third of adults under the age of thirty have outstanding student loan debt.

According to NerdWallet, April 2021, the debt elevator is going up!

Medicine	$201,490
Dental School	$292,169
Pharmacy School	$179,514
Veterinary School	$149,877
Average Graduate	$ 82,800

Solution:

Checkout this great resource, www.collegesimply.com for detailed college cost information.

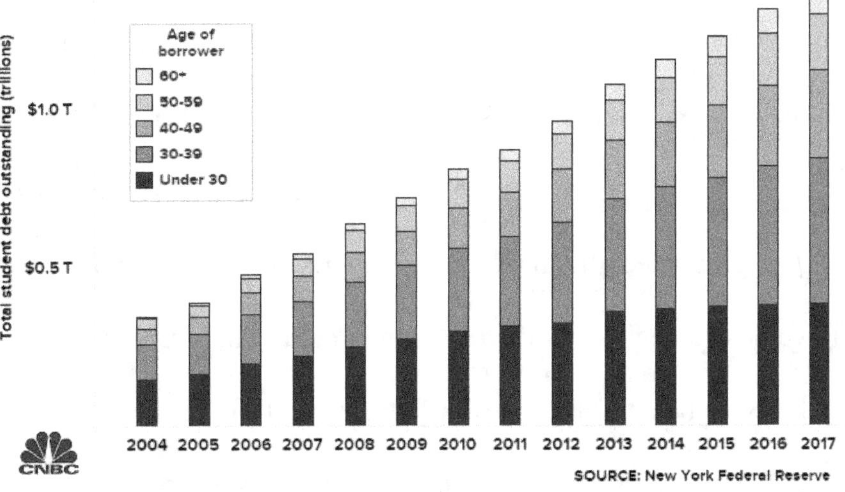

Parents: Discuss with your newly minted college student in advance how much access you, the parent, should have in their lives. Parents have no legal right to see their students' college transcripts. HIPPA rules block you from receiving any health information about your over-eighteen-years-of-age children, even if they are on your health care plan and you are paying the premiums. After they turn eighteen, they are 100% in charge of their finances. I suggest a Limited Power of Attorney (POW) signed by your eighteen-year-old child allowing you to have access to financial matters and a healthcare proxy for healthcare. This is insurance in case of an emergency.

Students: If you don't have a working relationship with your biological parents, consider giving limited "Power of Attorney" and your Healthcare Proxy to another trusted relative or friend. Just find someone trustworthy that will look out for your best interest.

https://www.forbes.com/sites/deborahljacobs/2014/08/15/two-documents-every-18-year-old-should-sign/#79c74d966e33

Step One for Applying to College: Fill out the required FAFSA form. This establishes your eligibility for financial aid. The form includes student and family income data from the parents. The FASFA form deadline is before the IRS April 15th tax return deadline, reinforcing the country's "Fire, Ready, Aim" mentality. Brace yourself, FASFA form completion is complicated and a pain in the neck. Enroll in your local Community College and save a ton of money. In Florida, if you graduate with an Associate of Arts degree, you may walk onto any Florida four-year university to begin your degree or major study in your junior year. Check to see if your state has the same benefit. That is what I did. I went to the amazing St. Johns River Community College in Palatka, Florida. It is on the top twenty list for least expensive colleges in the country! I'm honored to know I went to one of the cheapest colleges in the country!

When I graduated with my AA, I went to the University of North Florida to finish my business administration degree. I mostly lived at home when in Community College. When I went to UNF, I worked full time, and I went to school full time.

ROTC: Consider a military partnership while going to college. If you cannot afford a college education, ROTC programs can provide financial help while you attend the college of your choice. ROTC programs reward in more ways than financial ones. ROTC scholarships requires you to attend a military summer camp and complete four years of active duty. That is the price of admission.

Save in advance with a 529 plan.

Saving for college is a good idea. Although, saving for retirement is more important. The Coverdell Education Savings Account was the original program (ESA) was the original program. The Tax Cuts and Jobs Act of 2017 makes Coverdell redundant. State-sponsored 529 plans are now the "go to" tax benefit college savings plan.

In fact, 529 plans allow you to save for private K-12 tuition (up to $10,000) besides college expenses. A 529 plan named (like the 401k) after Section 529 of the Internal Revenue Code is a tax-advantaged plan of saving for your child's future college expenses. Individual states sponsor 529 savings plans. In Florida, for example, you open this "qualified" account and begin selecting investments that fit your investment style. Your child's future enrollment date chooses a target-style fund. The investment grows tax free like a traditional IRA. You should save automatically. You can ask your family and friends to contribute through an eGift portal. Use the 529 plan account for higher education expenses like tuition, fees, books and supplies. Use it for room and board. Use the funds for computers, peripherals, software and internet costs. The Florida plan allows you to attend any qualified educational institution nationwide or private. According to 529 plan requirements, your student must attend at least half-time in a program.

https://www.myfloridaprepaid.com/

Corporate Scholarships: My son and daughter received corporate scholarships. My son received a scholarship from Wachovia. My daughter received a scholarship from State Farm Insurance. Check with your employer about benefit availability.

Work-Study: Many, if not most colleges, offer work-study programs for students with financial need. The jobs are normally easy and still allow you time to work on classwork.

Grants: Free Money for Colleges

Unlike student loans, you do not repay grants! Most grants are need-based. The federal government provides grants. Your FASFA application will check your eligibility for government grants.

- Federal Pell Grants

- Federal Supplemental Education Opportunity Grants:

  https://studentaid.gov/understand-aid/types/grants/fseog

- State Grants http://www.collegescholarships.org/grants/state.htm Research your

  specific state for details.

- College Grants

- Popular Student-Specific Grants: Grants designed to aid the diverse array of students.

- TEACH Grants

- Military Grants

- Minority Specific Grants: African American, Hispanic, Native American, Asian

  American and Grants for Women

- Women's Colleges Offering Grants

- Industry Sponsored Grants: State Farm Insurance, National Society of Accountants,

  Future Farmers of America, Healthcare

- Grants for specific studies: See the Swann Foundation Fellowship for Caricature

  and Cartoons

- Grants for specific talents: Music, art, and photography grants

- Math Grants: National Science Foundation, American Math Society, Mu Alpha

  Theta, Raytheon

- Sports Grants: Play a sport? Get a grant.

There are hundreds of grant possibilities. You cannot be lazy. You cannot afford to be lazy. Put forth effort and apply for the grants. It's a good idea to add a nice photograph of yourself to the grant application.

Do the research and apply for as many grants as you can. Your current and future wallet will thank you. https://www.collegegrant.net/

Scholarships: There are many types of scholarships available.

- Academic Scholarships;

- Athletic Scholarships;

- Minority Scholarships;

- Scholarships for Women;

- Creative Scholarships;

- Scholarships from specific industries.

Start the scholarship application journey during the middle of your junior year in high school. Many scholarships ask for personal essays describing your dreams and aspirations. Learn to write well before you apply for scholarships. Scholarship applications have non-negotiable deadlines. Remember, deadlines are closer than they appear. Scholarship applications may need a photograph of you. Get photographed before starting the application journey. Research local businesses online to see if they offer scholarships. Electric companies, insurance companies, and any large businesses in your town may offer scholarships with no strings attached. Most civic organizations have scholarships. Apply to the Rotary, Kiwanis, Daughter of American Revolution, and Lion's Club.

Check out these scholarship research websites.

http://www.collegescholarships.org/financial-aid/

https://www.collegeboard.org/

https://bigfuture.collegeboard.org

https://www.fastweb.com/

Crowd Funding: Create a crowd funding post. https://www.gofundme.com/

Employer Reimbursement: I worked for Sprint Long Distance when I started my photography business. Sprint offered a generous tuition reimbursement package to employees. Several friends attended the local community college and received reimbursement. Likewise, State Farm Insurance has a college tuition reimbursement program. Check with your employer.

Raid Your IRA: I'm not a fan of this because parents should not sacrifice their retirement savings to finance your child's education. Please don't borrow from your traditional or Roth IRA to pay for college expenses without penalty. The IRS considers education a "qualified" reason, meaning that your fund raid is not subject to taxation. The IRS limits your borrowing to 50% of your vested account up to $50,000.

Student Loans: The Last Resort

Please check out www.studentloanhero.com. It is a division of Lending Tree. This site provides calculators and information about student loan financing.

There are three types of public federal student loans.

Direct Subsidized Loans	Direct Unsubsidized Loan	Direct PLUS Loan

➢ *For undergraduates*	➢ *For undergraduates,*	➢ *For parents to borrow*
➢ *Government*	*graduates, &*	*money in their own*
subsidizes the interest	*professional degrees*	*names to support*
on your loan, meaning	➢ *Fixed interest rates,*	*their child's education*
less owed money	*but higher for*	➢ *My least favorite*
➢ *Lender = Department*	*graduates*	➢ *Highest interest rate*
of Education (DOE)	➢ *Loan Limit = $20,500*	➢ *Requires clean credit*
➢ *Loan Limit = $5,500*	➢ *No credit check*	*rating*
➢ *Fixed Interest Rates*	➢ *Lender = Department*	
➢ *Income-based*	*of Education*	
repayment	➢ *Interest accumulates*	
➢ *No credit check*	*over time meaning it*	
	is unsubsidized	

- For undergraduates, the federal government subsidizes the Direct Subsidized Loan program. The federal government subsidizes the interest on your loan while you attend school, resulting in less money owed. The Department of Education is your lender. Establish financial need to qualify for this loan with a $5,500 limit. The advantages of a Federal Student Loan are fixed interest rates, income-based repayment, loan cancellation for specific careers (teach at a Title One School), and no credit check.

- The next federal student loan program is the Direct Unsubsidized Loan. Students can use this program for undergraduate, graduate, and professional degrees. Interest rates are fixed, but higher for graduate degrees. Interest accumulates during the entire period, hence unsubsidized. You can borrow up to $20,500. The Department of Education is the lender and collector. There is no credit check.

- The third federal program for loans is the Direct PLUS loan. This program is for parents to borrow money in their own name to support their child's education. This is my least favorite choice as it puts the parents on the hook. The Direct PLUS program has the highest interest rate of the three programs and requires a clean credit rating.

- After you exhaust government resources, the private student loan is the next option. Now we are back at the carnival. Many private student loan lenders use predatory lending tactics. The good news is that a few reputable private lenders exist. Students should not be shopping for private student loans until they exhaust every other source of funds for college. Suze Orman, famous financial guru, says: "Avoid private student loans at all costs."

- Discover

  - LendKey

- SallieMae

Cosigning: Be careful of lenders offering better rates with a co-signer. Cosigning is a plan destined to fail. A co-signer agrees to be 100% responsible for the debt. Guess what happens? The original borrower cannot pay and leaves you with the bill. One third of cosigned loans goes into default. Many private student loan companies allow the co-signer off the hook, officially called co-signer release, if the borrower satisfies the institution's payment rules. Institutions reject 90% of private student loan borrowers that apply for co-signer release. If your co-signer goes bankrupt, the lender can start an auto-default, even if the loan is in good standing. Demand for payment is immediate. You will have thirty days to pay off the loan. If you do not pay, you are in default. Hence the term auto-default. Word to the wise: don't cosign any loan or ask anyone to cosign your loan. It turns your college debt into a complicated legal matter. Speaking of the law, did you know that federal and private student loans are impossible to discharge in bankruptcy proceedings? That is why I say student loan debt takes priority over the rest of your debt.

Employers help Workers pay their Student Loan Debt

This Just In: Indentured Servitude

CNBC reports that income sharing agreements from colleges are taking shape. What are Income Sharing Agreements? Instead of paying your college education bills by borrowing money in  advance, you agree to have the college pay in advance for your education. In return, you agree to have a percentage of your future salary pay your college back for your education. Sounds great, right? Here is the catch: It may lead to unregulated philandering by college institutions receiving much more money in forfeited salary than if you just borrowed the money and paid the loan back with your paycheck. Most times, the ISA agreements ending up costing more than federal loans. The government may offer these programs. In a world of honest players, this method has merit. I am not a big fan of a government entity being responsible for deducting money from my paycheck to repay what is a debt. The fine print in the contracts included mandatory arbitration clauses, banned lawsuits, and may even force you to use a particular bank.

The world of college education financing is a veritable jungle. The unprepared student and parent stand to lose money. Be a frugal student and pick a high-quality, inexpensive community college for the first two years and live at home. When you graduate with your AA, pick another inexpensive, high-quality university that will satisfy your degree and future career needs. Ironically, after you receive your bachelor's degree, employers don't care about your alma mater. Employers basically care that you graduated from college. Many people have jobs that are not in their degree field. So, get out there and get your degree fast, furious, and as cheap as you can!

Retirees: Retirees owe $18.2 billion in student loan debt, a 650% increase from 2005.

Social Security offsets (garnishment) have increased over 500% (for over 40,000 people) for seniors 65 and older, according to AARP.

According to CBS News, three million Americans over the age of 60 still have student debt. The average debt was $33,800. Most incurred this debt while helping their children attend college. Other debt occurred when folks went back to school to enhance their job skills. The investment return on both scenarios failed a cost/benefit analysis.

Public Service Loan Forgiveness: This is another government program that sounds great when reported on the news, but in reality, is very difficult to qualify for. While you are in college, the regulations could change many times before you graduate. Consider it as "icing on the cake" if you receive this benefit.

Alternatives to Student Loan Debt

I never thought I would offer students alternatives to attending college. Here I am, a retired teacher, advocating college alternatives. One reason, according to the Washington Post, is that out of thousands of students graduating from college with desirable STEM degrees, 75 percent are working out of field. Why? There is a difference between the perception of what a STEM job entails and the reality. It does not seem to matter that there is an abundance of STEM jobs available. Second, an executive summary produced by Fidelity Investments reports 39% of the 2013 class would have made different choices related to college planning had they understood the true cost of college. Fifty percent of graduates would have researched more grants/scholarships. Sixty-nine percent of graduates said they could have cut back on eating out. Sixty-four percent of graduates said they could have cut back on retail spending. Third, seventy percent of the U.S. workforce does not have a degree.

Join the Military:

The current military experience is comparable to an apprenticeship. There are thousands of job possibilities available in military service. Remember, you serve and obey their orders and fill a need for the United States military. It is not a vacation. It is an honor to serve, but make sure you are mature enough to make an important decision. The military offers you training and careers in science, engineering, medicine, and communications. I have friends who started their military career serving as a corpsman (like a paramedic). Now, they are doctors practicing independently. Any job found in the world exists in the military. Regardless of the role you serve, the experience is helpful in the civilian world. Over one million veterans and their families take advantage of the G.I. bill's college benefits. There are ROTC programs that pay for your college and prepare you for an officer's role in the service in return for a service commitment period.

Go to Work:

There are many jobs that do not require a college education. Entry-level jobs offer the opportunity for advancement. My neighbor started in the stockroom at Walmart and is now a store manager. I have heard stories of entry-level workers in fast food restaurants becoming franchise owners. While possible, success requires hard work and long hours. Many organizations have call centers that need workers with no experience. The job involves sitting in a gray cubicle with a headset around your neck during your "tour" and assisting customers on the phone with their problems related to your industry. The work can be rewarding and pay well. Many companies offer tuition reimbursement. Be careful. I have friends and family that lost their entry-level customer service jobs because of technological advancements or because of outsourcing jobs overseas. I recommend starting your research for your dream job at https://www.bls.gov/ooh/home.htm. They pack this site with useful information. There is information about job salaries, education requirements, projected job numbers, and growth rate. Another going-to-work skill set you should master is learning the ins and outs of job search websites. Create a truthful and creative LinkedIn account. Be familiar with Glassdoor, Indeed, and Zip Recruiter. Plug in your resume and wait for responses. Plug in with sites such as Flex Jobs and Fiverr. These companies give you access to thousands of contract and freelance jobs. However, you should also be on the lookout for scams. Real employers do not ask you for money: period. Writing a paragraph on freelance work leads me to the next alternative.

Entrepreneurship:

Going into business is not for everyone. You must be self-motivated and require no supervision. You have a burning desire to succeed, and no one will stop you. If you meet these standards, then you discover that owning your own business is the most rewarding way to make a living. You will enjoy a sense of independence. There is no ceiling to the dollar amount of money you can earn. Did I mention no income floor, either? No regular paycheck, no guarantee your marketing will work, that your phone will ring, and no guarantee that Apple won't invent a device that destroys your business. Welcome to capitalism. The World of Creative Destruction. There is nothing like it in the world!

Success depends upon you finding and using mentors, getting a job in the field you wish to start a business in (what!), preparing for failure, and getting involved in theater. Shakespeare was right. "All the world is a stage." Do not be deliberately deceitful, but "Fake it until you make it" is a valid strategy. Join Toastmasters to excel at public speaking. You should have situational awareness. Recognize threats to your business model, current competitors, future competitors, and technical competitors. Pursue problems in your neighborhood. For example, I continually observe our nation's financial literacy shortcomings and this book is a response to that experience. Look for future opportunities. Make wise choices; always watch your back. Ideally, you will be successful. Failure is a success when you consider it a "learning experience."

https://www.entrepreneur.com/article/300403

Associate Degree:

If you are starting a career that needs more than a high school education, but less than a bachelor's degree, consider an associate degree. There are three main types of associate degrees:

The Associate of Arts degree is a general education degree to prepare you for the University experience. An Associate of Science degree prepares you for a special career. You can still transfer to a university, but an Associate of Science degree prepares you for the workforce. Types of jobs include:

Air Traffic Controller;

Computer Programmer;

Web Developer;

Law Enforcement;

Automobile Repair Technician;

Engineering Technician;

Medical Imaging Technician.

There is also the Associate in Applied Science. This category is more job specific, thus the Associate in Applied Science provides training in accounting, web design, nursing, paralegal respiratory care and teaching assistant.

Trade Schools

Trade schools prepare you for many careers. According to the National Association of State Directors of Technical Education Consortium, there are seventy-nine career pathways within sixteen vocational divisions. Career Tech Education in high schools and colleges provided training for specific careers.

The most popular career training paths include:

- Personal care aides;

- Home health aides;

- Diagnostic medical sonographers;

- Occupational therapy assistants;

- Cosmetology;

- Dental hygienists;

- Medical equipment repairers;

- Medical assistants;

- Licensed practical and licensed vocational nurses. Don't forget to consider the construction trades. Many people enjoy working with their hands. Trade Schools can prepare students for electrical, heavy equipment operation, carpentry, plumbing, and welding careers. Good automobile mechanics are hard to find. Individuals with entrepreneurial acumen can gain more financial rewards by opening their own shops.

Apprenticeships and Internships

An apprenticeship is a paid, on-the-job, training program that results in industry certification and sometimes an Associate of Arts degree.

Please watch this video to understand the role of apprenticeships in a dynamic workforce.

https://www.youtube.com/watch?v=BU1w-yxQw1k

A significant advantage to the apprenticeship strategy is the opportunity to receive your education, an Associate degree at no charge. Besides that, you will also get industry certifications and a full-time job offer. This website describes the BMW program.

BMW Apprenticeships

Are you a Disney "Phile"?

https://www.disneyanimation.com/careers/interns-apprentices

Do you love Universal Studios?

https://jobs.universalparks.com/universal-orlando-resort/life-at-universal-orlando/

Also look into Google Universal Internships. Internships may be handled by third party online employment agencies like Indeed.

Are you a "Space Nut"?   https://intern.nasa.gov/

Plumbing?   Apollo Home

Culinary Arts?   Boyd Gaming   BoydCareers

Finance?   Fidelity Investments

Customer Service?   Enterprise Rental Car

Technology?   Aon

An apprenticeship lasts between one and five years.

An internship is a shorter experience lasting three to six months. Internships can be "paid" or "unpaid," and concentrate on career investigation. Internships do not result in certification. An internship is a long-term job shadowing experience. Students affiliated with a college in a paid internship opportunity received a job offer 60% of the time. Unpaid internships offer an opportunity for you to shine in front of a potential employer. Unpaid internships act as a long-term interview, allowing you to prove your worth.

https://www.thebalancecareers.com/what-is-an-internship-1986729

Student Loan Alternative Reality

I ask: Why don't the banks require borrowers to produce their personal budgets? Loan applications ask for income, then, why don't student loan lenders ask for or prepare a working budget for their student borrower? In fact, colleges should hire a full-time financial coaches to teach students how to make wise decisions about spending their student loan proceeds. They could give seminars to incoming freshman (who, three months before were high school seniors) teaching the students about money management. Is this revolutionary thinking? Part of me thinks the lenders would not be happy lending less money to students who may behave more responsibly. It might be bad for business.

Is this quote an endorsement for Get WalletWise?

"Many kids come out of college, they have a credit card and a diploma. They don't know how to buy a house or a car or health insurance or life insurance. They do not know basic microeconomics." ~ Jesse Jackson

Summary Questions

Exercise Time: *minimum 20 minutes*

Please answer these questions. Revisit your answers later, after you've started implementing the lessons in this chapter, to see if you feel differently about student loan debt.

I. *If you knew you could not fail, what would you want to accomplish in your life. Make your dream first person, specific, and brief.*

II. *a. Are your parents helping you with your college decision prior to you enrolling in college? Are you going lone wolf?*

III. *b. Are you the first generation in your family to go to college?*

IV. *Do you think you have the emotional maturity to make complex financial and life decisions alone? If not, who are you going to call?*

V. *Do you think student loans are setting students up for failure in life? Answer this question from your perspective.*

VI. *Why do you think it takes students 6 years to complete a four-year program?*

VII.   *a. Are you comfortable applying for college scholarships? What information will you need to fill out the scholarship applications? b. What scholarships are you thinking about applying to?*

VIII.   *How do you feel about the idea of your student loans being covered by your employer in exchange for a minimum time of service to that company? How could you calculate the total cost to compare if it is a good deal?*

IX.   *What are the advantages to joining the military?*

X.   *FAFSA is a difficult document to complete. Download a copy to review. <u>FAFSA Form</u> Who will help you fill out the FASFA form?*

A short task

I. *In many college and scholarship applications, there is a requirement to write an essay. To prepare for this, write a short 250-400 word essay about student loans. This assignment helps you evaluate student loans from your perspective and prepare you for the future essays you may write.*

II. *Go to https://www.consumerfinance.gov/consumer-tools/student-loans/ and research the student loan resources.*

Define:

*Co-signer*____

*Subsidized Loan*____

*Work Study*____

*Federal Student Loans*____

III. *Watch the video, Everyone has a story. Meet Dani, and discuss in class how Dani felt about her private student debt. What happened after she filed a complaint with the CFPB?*

Chapter 3

Gambling and Lotto

"Divorce, loss of productivity, bankruptcy,

and crime are only a few of the many consequences that can occur."

–Gamblinghelp.org

On this bombshell, The Supreme Court, in 2018, allowed states to legalize sports gambling.

Online sports gambling surged during the pandemic because most people had nothing productive

to do. According to a major research firm prediction, by 2027, the online gambling market will

be worth 127 billion dollars. The major casinos are changing the casino floor to make gambling

more appealing to millennials. They prefer a more video game-like experience, called iGaming,

than the old-fashioned slot machines. Casinos are scrambling to cater to the new customers. If

you are spending $1.00 per week on your state lottery, I am not worried about you. However,

know what is happening in your surrounding culture. Gambling is almost never a good idea.

The "Lootery" (Play on Words)

My wife, while driving home from a trip to Tampa, stopped at a convenience store to get a

bottled water. What she saw in the convenience store was interesting. There was a line of tired

workers ready to buy their lotto tickets. Apparently, the jackpot rose to an amount that attracted

more players than usual. Yes, it is their right to buy a lotto tickets and play these "games" for

entertainment. It saddens me, though, that most of them do not realize they are wasting their

money. To worsen matters, a lot of good people think playing the lottery is a legitimate

retirement planning strategy!

The investment app Stash commissioned an online survey of 1,156 people and found that about forty percent of American consumers who responded, including fifty-nine percent of millennials, think winning the lottery could be a good way to fund retirement. What's more interesting is that nearly one in four millennials surveyed said they're actually basing their retirement plans from winning the lottery.

https://www.annuity.org/2019/05/30/banking-on-the-lottery-to-fund-retirement/

It is also common knowledge that gambling can cause difficulties in one's home life, financial life, career, and general health.

The odds of matching three numbers and winning $5.00 are one in seventy. That means you will spend $70 to win $5.00. Please understand that the risk against reward ratio for playing the lotto or any other game of chance is working against you. You will almost always lose money.

Most people with a winning "scratch off" ticket will use winnings to buy more scratch off tickets until they own only losing tickets.

https://www.lotto.net/florida-lotto/prizes

The Florida Lottery sponsored a demographic survey by *Ipsos* that stated that the largest segment of players (33% of total lottery revenue) was the youngest segment. 37% of players are 18-34. They are also the least educated with 27% having high school diplomas or less. This segment has the highest participation in other gaming such as Bingo, raffles, Jai Alai, and "I" gaming (online gaming).

https://www.flalottery.com/exptkt/FloridaSegmentationFinalReport.pdf

I suspect these players think their lotto dollars will support "education." It's like an investment…………………………

Where does the lotto money go? See this cheerful advertising piece that the Florida Lottery created. So warm and fuzzy! http://www.flalottery.com/whereMoneyGoes

Is there a discrepancy here? The Florida Legislature created lotto in 1986, under the condition that lotto proceeds were funding the Educational Enhancement Trust Fund (EETF) and used to ENHANCE education. Their literature clearly states most revenue goes to pay prize winners and to pay commissions to the vendors.

How do you feel about gambling?

Do you think gambling or lotto is/would be fun? What makes it fun?

How often do you gamble?

How do you feel after gambling? And how do you feel if you lose?

How could gambling increase the risk of bankruptcy in your life?

According to the Sun-Sentinel November 29, 2018:

"If there's nefarious activity going on here, it's not that lottery money isn't going to education-related budget items, but that it's not supplementing education funding. It's supplanting it."
"Also, the state has other budget priorities, such as healthcare and criminal justice, says Cheryl Etters, spokeswoman for Florida's education department." [2]

This means the old shell game affects another part of our prized education budget. They use the lotto money more and more for running day-to-day Florida government operations.

With my interest in education in mind, I noted that gambling addiction affects the full spectrum of the population, not just the disheveled laborer. The website www.gamblinghelp.org has a research department that lists materials and studies about middle and High School Students!

Quote: "In brief: gambling is a widespread fact of life among middle and high school students in Florida. More than half of the students surveyed reported gambling during the last twelve months. Even assuming that recreational gambling is harmless, the data consistently shows a straight-line correlation ranging from students who do not gamble to those who may gamble very little, to those who are high-risk gamblers for all items analyzed. The high-risk gamblers are the most likely to have higher use rates of alcohol, drugs, and tobacco; struggle with depression; engage in antisocial behaviors; have trouble in school; have more risk factors and fewer protective factors."—Dr. Louis Lieberman, Dr. Mary Cuadrado June 2006.

Chronic gambling is prevalent in the arrestee community. Folks gamble with borrowed money. Folks gamble with their government assistance payments, and there is a college student gambling problem in Florida.

So, in conclusion, let's list the achievements of lotto.

1. Entry level game leading to chronic addiction. CHECK.

2. Increasing income inequality among uneducated, young citizens. CHECK.

3. Providing false hope for the least among us. CHECK.

4. Use the funds to skirt a balanced budget amendment by mis-allocating education funds. CHECK.

5. Create another distraction to success by middle school, high school, and college students. CHECK

6. Develop advertisements directed at the poor. CHECK.

7. Develop false advertising focusing on the public good of buying a lottery ticket. CHECK.

8. Create another stumbling block for citizens as a personal budget buster affecting lifelong finances. CHECK.

9. Create a financial/political predatory monster that can never be reversed, as the state treasury needs your money! CHECK.

10. Underage Gambling. **CHECKMATE.**

Instead

The average American spends almost $220 per year on lottery tickets. Invest that amount in an investment that models the S & P 500 like the SPDR S&P ETF. After 20 years, you could accumulate $10,000.

See this link for a humorous look at lottery life:

https://www.jonathanpond.com/lotteries

Better yet, you can save $100 per month in an S & P 500 index fund. If you earn a conservative 7%, you will have accumulated $240,000 after 40 years. That is a sound investment plan. Gambling is not a sound investment plan.

Please read Chapter Eight: Saving and Investing.

Additional Resources:

[1]   https://govinfo.library.unt.edu/ngisc/research/lotteries.html

[2]   https://www.jacksonville.com/news/metro/2016-04-07/story/florida-gets-f-new-school-funding-report

[3]   https://lawecommons.luc.edu/cgi/viewcontent.cgi?article=1964&context=lclr

Legitimate Lottery Concerns as a Winner

Easy Come, Easy Go.

Most winners of the lotto and other large money jackpots consider winning a curse! I base the following discussion on my research of lottery winners' stories and events.

Why do you say that winning money is a curse? Your friends will take advantage of you.

Believe it.

Expect to have a lot of new friends if you win the lottery. I am not against anyone winning the lottery, but if most Americans are financially illiterate, the chances are good that the winner of a lottery jackpot cannot manage his or her winnings. Dozens of stories describe the tragic events related to winning the lottery. If I were the king, lotto winners would come with a highly paid advisor with the sole purpose of teaching money management to reduce the possibility that they will lose their fortune. Remember, you only have to become rich once. The goal after you become rich is not to lose your fortune. It is an enormous task emotionally to manage a large sum of money properly. Become effective at working with attorneys, accountants, financial advisors, and bankers. Newsflash! Not all are honest or looking out for your best interest. I watched from a distance as a group of real estate brokers defrauded a working-class client who inherited a large sum of money because of an industrial accident. The money flowed rapidly from client to real estate brokers! My advice to you is to seek a disinterested party who can refer you to an honest, professional advisor.

A lot of money can damage your relationship.

Your risk of bankruptcy will increase. Because you do not know how to manage money, bankers will aggressively tell you, "You've got great credit!" You borrow money under the idea that you have plenty of money to pay it back! Who needs a budget? I'm loaded.

Your family members and the long-lost relatives will come out of the woodwork with the most creative "down on my luck" stories that only you can solve with your newfound money.

Here are some links to support this discussion.

https://www.yahoo.com/video/5-reasons-dont-want-win-170450079.html It must be an outstanding feeling to check the numbers on your favorite legal game of chance and see that you have won the jackpot! Congratulations! The odds of winning the Florida Lotto jackpot are about 1:23,000,000. In Florida, the probability of getting struck by lightning in your lifetime is 1 in 3000. That means as a winner of Lotto you have (probably) been struck by lightning 7600 times before you won your prize.

The sad story of Jack Whittaker was all over the news in 2012 for winning almost $315 million dollars back in 2002. His granddaughter and daughter died soon after from drug overdoses. They robbed him of excessive amounts of cash multiple times, and they hacked his bank accounts, according to one report. He was being sued by Caesar's Atlantic for unpaid gambling debts.

A very sad story involves Abraham Shakespeare, who won the Florida lottery in 2009 to the tune of $30 million dollars. He was murdered soon afterward by a new girlfriend who a jury found guilty of first-degree murder in 2012.

How about Georgia native, Ronnie Music Jr., sentenced to 21 years in prison for investing in a crystal methamphetamine "business?"

And the stories go on and on.

The stories detail financial tragedy, rags to riches back to rags stories, murder, suicide, bankruptcy, arguments with coworkers, drug addictions, lawsuits, IRS fights and more. Is this what the "government" calls protecting its citizens? It's another nightmare placed upon an unknowing and vulnerable public to pay for ever-expanding government budgets.

If you win the lottery, immediately protect your identity and try to stay anonymous. There are only six states that allow you to protect your anonymity. The government wants the money spread around like flying fertilizer, regardless of if the windfall destroys your life. Don't sign your ticket. Just remember, though, if you lose an unsigned ticket, someone else can find it and legally redeem it. If you sign your ticket early, it may prevent you from setting up the blind trust you need. Make copies of the ticket for your attorney and accountant. Lock the original ticket in a safe place. You should contact a trustworthy attorney as soon as possible to set up a trust. Take your time. There is a window and rushing to the lottery office is not a good idea. Set up a new post office box address and phone number to give to the press. Put together your crack team of financial advisors, bankers, attorneys, and accountants. You may hire a public relations specialist. Ask your attorney for a reference. You have become a rockstar!

Consider surrounding yourself with close family, friends, clergy, and professional counselors to keep your sanity.

Why do people win multimillion-dollar lotteries only to return to their original net worth or worse? They had no system in place to handle and manage an enormous amount of money. They end up returning to the place they began before winning the prize: broke.

Sports Gambling

Recently, Americans did not approve of sports gambling. After the government stepped in saying they will regulate the business of sports gambling, there came a change of heart. The average citizen thought more tax revenue from sports gambling businesses results in less taxes owed by him or her. Now, Americans approve of sports gambling online. The Supreme Court reversed 100 years of sports gambling opposition in the 2018 Murphy v. NCAA case. The decision gives states the authority to regulate sports gambling within their states. Ironically, the decision came nearly 100 years after the 1919 Black Sox Baseball Scandal.

Like pornography and drug addictions, gambling stimulates the same pleasure centers. Your brain sees a cue that predicts a reward. The cue could be a lottery ticket commercial or an advertisement for an online sports gambling site, and you see dollar signs floating in front of you. You respond to this stimulus by buying a lottery ticket or placing a bet online. If you win, you are hooked. You have just programmed your brain through a craving process to repeat the cycle. The human brain knows how to survive in the jungle, and this thought cycle is great for survival in the "real jungle," but not so much in the "modern" jungle.

I just reviewed one of the large online sports gambling sites and looked at the statistics involved in gambling. If you can understand those calculations, get a job as an actuary, accountant, or financial advisor.

If you win a large lottery, CNBC money guru Jim Cramer suggests doing this:

1. Do not invest in anything risky;
2. Take the Lump Sum, pay the taxes now while tax rates are low;
3. Invest in Treasury Bonds;
4. Buy valuable real estate to fight against hyperinflation;
5. Invest in Precious Metals;
6. Invest in High Quality Art;
7. Invest 5% in Bitcoin;
8. Invest in Municipal Bonds;
9. Invest in Dividend-Paying Stocks.

In Conclusion:

If you gamble for entertainment, consider investing the money in legitimate assets. If you are spending $1.00 a week on a lotto ticket, I am not worried about you. However, know what is happening in the surrounding culture. Gambling is almost never a good idea. The big casino, online sports businesses, and state lotto provides inventive addictive environments to attract you to their venue. They hope you will stay. They do not care if you lose all of your money. To them, that is not their concern. They do not care about your finances, and it is a legal way for them to make money for them. Their single goal is to make as much money for their business as possible, and they do not care how many lives they ruin in their quest for profits.

Chapter 3

Student Loans

Summary Questions

Exercise Time: Approximately 20 minutes

I. *In your own words, describe the difference between casino gambling and buying lotto tickets?*

II. *What is your opinion on sports gambling? Do you have a favorite team and sport that might motivate you to gamble?*

III. *Do you consider the idea of depending on games of chance or luck as entertainment or a way to make money?*

IV. *Explain why or why not: Is gambling a good retirement strategy?*

V. *How can you avoid gambling? Is it self-control? Fear? Observing others?*

VI. *Should gambling be legalized in your state? If so, how do you predict this will affect people who have never gambled?*

VII. *Do you think gambling is an investment? What is the difference between an investment and gambling? Whether yes/no, please state your reasons for saying so!*

VIII.   Does everyone who wins a large lottery prize live happily ever after? Why or why not?

Quick Task!

Check out the website for Gambler's Anonymous and answer the questions to see if you are a

compulsive gambler: https://www.gamblersanonymous.org/ga/content/20-questions

If you have a gambling problem, please call 1-888-ADMIT-IT (263-4848) or checkout the

website: www.gamblinghelp.org

Or, https://www.addictions.com/gambling/

Chapter 4

Money Management and Your Budget

"Having a plan with money doesn't just help you right now,

it also gives you hope for the end goal."

—Dave Ramsey

A budget is the most important tool to achieve financial responsibility and ultimate success. It helps you from becoming a victim of financial fraud, bank errors, predatory sales, and predatory lenders. Ironically, ignorance of your finances will reduce your freedom and future opportunities. Budgets are liberators! Ignorance of your finances may cause calls from collection agents. These are calls are a nuisance and take away from your preferred activities.

Approximately 40% of Americans keep track of their finances through the use of a budget, according to a study by U.S. Bank. Another study by Career Builder in 2017 showed only 32% of respondents used a budget. One purpose of this book is to increase that percentage and help you keep track of your hard-earned dollars. The point is: please create and use your budget as the best tool to reach financial independence. Don't worry about what other folks are not doing.

I know it is work, but anything worth having (like money bliss) is worth the effort.

Let's begin our meeting with your money. You know, a money date!

A Six-Step Plan to Understand and Take Ownership of Your Finances:

This plan summarizes the steps to become financially literate.

Step 1: Establish a $1,000 Emergency Fund. This may sound like a bad first step if you are in serious money trouble, but save $100 per month for ten months and you're there. An emergency fund reduces your dependence on your credit card as a piggy bank.

1. Create a real budget and a balance sheet on paper (I discuss detailed steps below).

2. Check your Credit Reports. See Chapter Five: Check your Credit Reports and Credit Scores.

3. Open a Mint Account (this is a budget app that lives on your phone and computer) that helps you track your money in total.

4. Track and reduce expenses on paper.
    a) Sell expensive assets and use cash to repay debt.
    b) Trim gift expenses (Birthday and Holiday gifts can be budget busters).
    c) Take Inexpensive Vacations.

5. Receive better prices on bulk necessities you always purchase by joining a warehouse club, like BJ's, Costco, or Sam's.

6. Increase income (take on a sustainable side hustle) Make extra money with a side hustle.

Step 2: Pay off debt. The "Snowball" method pays the lowest balances first. The Avalanche method pays the highest rate first.

1. Credit Cards.

2. Personal Notes.

3. Store Accounts.

4. You can refinance your car at your credit union at a lower interest rate. If you are in serious financial problems, you may have to sell the expensive "high payment" car to remove the expensive car payment obligation and buy a car for cash. (Please see Chapter Seven: Automobiles, to learn how to find a good car you can buy with cash.

Step 3: Establish Complete Emergency Fund $20,000.

Step 4: Retirement Planning:

1. Start saving ten percent of net income after the emergency fund is complete.

2. Fund your 401k enough to qualify for company match.

3. Increase retirement savings to fifteen percent of net income.

4. Open a Roth IRA after you max out 401k match.

5. Max out IRA Contributions.

Step 5: Save for a College 529 Plan, Open a savings account in the child's name.

Step 6: Payoff your mortgage or buy an affordable house with an affordable mortgage.

Time for a Budget!

To access the Budget, Expense Tracker and Net Worth/Balance Sheet templates, please see https://www.walletwise.org/downloadableresources. Click on the XLS file you need to pop it open. Your interactive selection will open in Microsoft Excel.

I created these original resources for you. There are step-by-step examples below to show you how to use them. The Excel file automatically adds and subtracts for you. If you have any difficulty accessing these resources, email me at kenremsen@walletwise.org and I will email you the forms.

1. **List Your Income**

The income portion asks for net income after taxes. I did this to simplify the budget from having a separate category for taxes.

If your income is in commission style, inconsistent, month-to-month, or you are self-employed, then use your annual income and divide it by twelve. Do not consider business expense reimbursements as income.

2. **List Your Estimated Expenses**

I've designed a budget with thirteen different expense categories. Please take the time to list your expenses accurately. Each section should total each category automatically.

Estimate any expense that does not occur monthly by taking your annual expense of a particular item and dividing it by twelve. The budget will total your expenses and subtract them from your income to calculate your "Surplus" (YEAH!) or "Deficit" (BOO!)

I attempted to place the categories in order of importance on a normal budget. Yes, that's right, if you have a balanced budget, charitable giving comes first.

3.   Check the Percentages

Please keep in mind that the expense percentages are just a recommendation. Folks with different incomes will experience different percentages. Oh! The guidelines do not add up to 100%. It's like the pirate's code; they are just guidelines. The guideline for credit card and unsecured debt is 0%, but, that is rarely the case.

As an additional resource, Dave Ramsey suggests there are roughly ten categories for budgeting: housing (25-35%), food (10-15%), transportation (10-15%), insurance (10-25%), utilities (5-10%), health (5-10%), recreational (5-10%), personal (10-15%), giving (10-15%), and saving (10-15%). Compare these percentages to yours to see how you rate.

The key is to spend less than you earn.

Budgeting in a Nutshell

Before starting the Excel worksheet, consider separating your expense into three clean categories. The 50/30/20 rule is a simple way to get started. 50% of your monthly take-home (net income) goes to essential expenses. These essential expenses include rent/mortgage, food, car payments/insurance, debt payments, court debts and utilities. 30% of your budget goes to discretionary (fun) expenses, and 20% of your budget goes into savings. Personally, I would only use this as an overview of your budget. Many famous budget pundits encourage this method. I don't. This method does not help you manage your money. It is what I call, a rule of thumb.

I know you can develop the discipline to take an hour of your time and write all of your income and expenses on a few sheets of paper. You will thank yourself later for doing the hard work now instead of taking the easy way out.

<table>
<tr><td colspan="3">WalletWise Monthly Budget</td><td></td></tr>
<tr><td>Date of Plan:</td><td></td><td></td><td></td></tr>
<tr><td>Your Name:</td><td></td><td></td><td></td></tr>
<tr><td colspan="3">Monthly Net Income</td><td></td></tr>
<tr><td>Description</td><td>Amount</td><td></td><td></td></tr>
<tr><td>Monthly Salary</td><td></td><td></td><td></td></tr>
<tr><td>Child Support / Alimony (Income)</td><td></td><td></td><td></td></tr>
<tr><td>Interest Income</td><td></td><td></td><td></td></tr>
<tr><td>Side Hustle 1</td><td></td><td></td><td></td></tr>
<tr><td>Side Hustle 2</td><td></td><td></td><td></td></tr>
<tr><td>Commissions</td><td></td><td></td><td></td></tr>
<tr><td>Retirement Income</td><td></td><td></td><td></td></tr>
<tr><td>Net Business Income</td><td></td><td></td><td></td></tr>
<tr><td>Other Income</td><td></td><td></td><td></td></tr>
<tr><td>Income Total</td><td>0.00</td><td></td><td></td></tr>
</table>

<table>
<tr><td colspan="3">Monthly Expenses</td><td>Percentage</td></tr>
<tr><td>A. Donations and Gifts</td><td>Amount</td><td></td><td></td></tr>
<tr><td>Local Charity or Local Church</td><td></td><td>Guideline 12%</td><td></td></tr>
<tr><td>Gifts (Birthdays)</td><td></td><td>Your %</td><td>0</td></tr>
<tr><td>Gifts (Christmas)</td><td></td><td>Over / Under</td><td>-12.00</td></tr>
<tr><td>Gift Total</td><td>0.00</td><td></td><td></td></tr>
</table>

<table>
<tr><td>B. Savings and Investment</td><td>Amount</td><td></td><td></td></tr>
<tr><td>Emergency Savings</td><td></td><td></td><td></td></tr>
<tr><td>Auto Replacement Savings</td><td></td><td></td><td></td></tr>
<tr><td>401k/403b Retirement Plans</td><td>0</td><td></td><td></td></tr>
<tr><td>IRA</td><td></td><td>Guideline 5%</td><td></td></tr>
<tr><td>College Funds</td><td></td><td>Your %</td><td>0</td></tr>
<tr><td>Stocks / Bonds</td><td></td><td>Over / Under</td><td>-5.00</td></tr>
<tr><td>Financial Total</td><td>0.00</td><td></td><td></td></tr>
</table>

<table>
<tr><td>C. Home</td><td>Amount</td><td></td><td></td></tr>
<tr><td>Mortgage</td><td></td><td></td><td></td></tr>
<tr><td>Property Tax</td><td>.</td><td></td><td></td></tr>
<tr><td>Homeowners/Flood Insurance</td><td></td><td></td><td></td></tr>
<tr><td>Rent</td><td></td><td></td><td></td></tr>
<tr><td>Renters Insurance</td><td></td><td>Guideline 27%</td><td></td></tr>
<tr><td>Pest Control / Termite Bond</td><td></td><td>Your %</td><td>0</td></tr>
<tr><td>Lawn Pest Control / Other</td><td></td><td>Over / Under</td><td>-27.00</td></tr>
<tr><td>Home Total</td><td>0.00</td><td></td><td></td></tr>
</table>

D. Utility	Amount			
Electricity				
Water / Sewer				
Mobile Telephone				
TV / Cable / Satellite/ Internet			Guideline 3%	
Heat Gas / Oil			Your %	0
Other			Over / Under	-3.00
	Utilities Total	0.00		

E. Food	Amount			
Groceries			Guideline 7%	
Eating Out			Your %	0
Vitamins & Supplements			Over / Under	-7.00
	Utilities Total	0.00		

F. Auto/ Transportation	Amount			
Car Payments				
Auto Insurance				
Fuel				
Uber/Lyft				
Repairs/Maintenance/Tire			Guideline 7%	
AAA/Auto Club			Your %	0
OnStar / Satellite Radio			Over / Under	-7.00
	Auto Total	0.00		

G. Credit Cards & Debt	Amount			
Credit Card 1				
Credit Card 2				
Store Credit Card			Guideline 0%	
Gas Credit Card			Your %	0
Unsecured Consumer Debt			Over / Under	0.00
	Auto Total	0.00		

H. Health and Fitness	Amount			
Doctor				
Dentist				
Prescriptions				
Eye Glasses / Contacts				
Deductibles				
HAS / Flexible Spending Accounts			Guideline 5%	
Gym Membership			Your %	0
			Over / Under	-5.00
	Health Total	0.00		

I. Insurance	Amount			
Health Insurance				
Dental Insurance				
Vision Insurance				
Disability Insurance			Guideline 7%	
Life Insurance			Your %	0
Long-Term Care Insurance			Over / Under	-7.00
	Insurance Total	0.00		

J. Children	Amount			
Child Care				
Baby Sitting			Guideline 4%	
Kids Allowance			Your %	0
Music / Dance Lessons			Over / Under	-4.00
	Children Total	0.00		

K. Personal Care	Amount			
Hair Care				
Toiletries / Cosmetics				
Tax Preparation				
Sports / Hobbies				
Subscriptions / Dues			Guideline 6%	
Clothes			Your %	0
Laundry / Dry Cleaning			Over / Under	-6.00
	Personal Care Total	0.00		

L. Pets	Amount			
Pet Food & Supplies				
Veterinarian			Guideline 1%	
Boarding /Pet Sitting			Your %	0
Pet Insurance			Over / Under	-1.00
	Pets Total	0.00		

M. Travel	Amount			
Vacation Motel / Food			Guideline 2%	
Rental Car			Your %	0
Unexpected Travel			Over / Under	-2.00
	Travel Total	0.00		

Monthly	Net Spendable Income	0.00
Monthly	Total Expenses	0.00
Monthly	**Budget Surplus or Deficit**	**0.00**

Here is a sample budget with a typical income and expenses based on U.S. statistics of personal income and expenses.

Sample WalletWise Monthly Budget			
Date of Plan:	1/1/2021		
Your Name:			
Monthly Net Income			
Description	Amount		
Monthly Salary	5000		
Child Support / Alimony (Income)			
Interest Income			
Side Hustle 1	200		
Side Hustle 2			
Commissions			
Retirement Income			
Net Business Income			
Other Income			
Income Total	**5200.00**		

Monthly Expenses			Percentage
A. Donations and Gifts	Amount		
Local Charity or Local Church	100		Guideline 12%
Gifts (Birthdays)	200		Your % — 11.54
Gifts (Christmas)	300		Over / Under — -0.46
Gift Total	**600.00**		

B. Savings and Investment	Amount		
Emergency Savings	100		
Auto Replacement Savings	100		
401k/403b Retirement Plans	100		
IRA			Guideline 5%
College Funds			Your % — 5.77
Stocks / Bonds			Over / Under — 0.77
Financial Total	**300.00**		

C. Home	Amount		
Mortgage	842		
Property Tax	140		
Homeowners/Flood Insurance	120		
Rent			
Renters Insurance			Guideline 27%
Pest Control / Termite Bond	40		Your % — 21.96
Lawn Pest Control / Other			Over / Under — -5.04
Home Total	**1142.00**		

D. Utility	Amount			
Electricity	125			
Water / Sewer	40			
Mobile Telephone	118			
TV / Cable / Satellite/ Internet	120		Guideline 3%	
Heat Gas / Oil			Your %	7.75
Other			Over / Under	4.75
Utilities Total	**403.00**			

E. Food	Amount			
Groceries	500		Guideline 7%	
Eating Out			Your %	9.62
Vitamins & Supplements			Over / Under	2.62
Food Total	**500.00**			

F. Auto/ Transportation	Amount			
Car Payments	568			
Auto Insurance	120			
Fuel				
Uber/Lyft				
Repairs/Maintenance/Tire	25		Guideline 7%	
AAA/Auto Club	10		Your %	13.90
OnStar / Satellite Radio			Over / Under	6.90
Auto Total	**723.00**			

G. Credit Cards & Debt	Amount			
Credit Card 1	250			
Credit Card 2	250			
Store Credit Card			Guideline 14%	
Gas Credit Card			Your %	14.42
Unsecured Consumer Debt	250		Over / Under	0.42
Credit Card Total	**750.00**			

H. Health and Fitness	Amount			
Doctor	40			
Dentist	20			
Prescriptions	75			
Eye Glasses / Contacts	25			
Deductibles	50			
HSA / Flexible Spending Accounts			Guideline 5%	
Gym Membership			Your %	4.04
			Over / Under	-0.96
Health Total	**210.00**			

I. Insurance	Amount			
Health Insurance	75			
Dental Insurance	25			
Vision Insurance				
Disability Insurance			Guideline 7%	
Life Insurance			Your %	1.92
Long-Term Care Insurance			Over / Under	-5.08
Insurance Total		**100.00**		

J. Children	Amount			
Child Care	500			
Baby Sitting			Guideline 4%	
Kids Allowance			Your %	9.62
Music / Dance Lessons			Over / Under	5.62
Children Total		**500.00**		

K. Personal Care	Amount			
Hair Care	45			
Toiletries / Cosmetics				
Tax Preparation	10			
Sports / Hobbies	10			
Subscriptions / Dues			Guideline 6%	
Clothes			Your %	1.25
Laundry / Dry Cleaning			Over / Under	-4.75
Personal Care Total		**65.00**		

L. Pets	Amount			
Pet Food & Supplies				
Veterinarian			Guideline 1%	
Boarding /Pet Sitting			Your %	0
Pet Insurance			Over / Under	-1.00
Pets Total		**0.00**		

M. Travel	Amount			
Vacation Motel / Food			Guideline 2%	
Rental Car			Your %	0
Unexpected Travel			Over / Under	-2.00
Travel Total		**0.00**		
				1.79

Monthly	Net Spendable Income	5200.00	
Monthly	Total Expenses	5293.00	
Monthly	**Budget Surplus or Deficit**	**-93.00**	

You may discover that you spend more than you make. It's time to make tough decisions to get your expenses less than your income. Cancel cable, gym memberships, stop eating out, and whatever else it takes to turn your budget around.

I did not include a separate category for income tax because we used net (after tax) income.

1.   **Track Expenses**

Regardless of the budget plan you decide to use, it will be necessary to track and record all expenditures for thirty days. It's difficult. It is certainly not fun. You need to do this; however, to get a handle on what and where you are spending your money. Make a copy of the expense tracker and take it with you daily to mark down your expenses. I keep all of my receipts of the day and add them to the tracker at one time.

Procedure: Each time you spend money, record the amount in the correct spending category, A through M. The budget items match the expense sheet items.

Download the Worksheet: https://www.walletwise.org/downloadableresources

Look for WalletWise Expense Tracker and click on the XLS file.

WalletWise Expense Tracking

							Budget					0
				% Spent	-	-	-	-	-	-	-	-
				Remaining	-	-	-	-	-	-	-	-

Date	Payment Type	Description	Gift & Donation	Savings & Invest	Home	Utility	Food	Auto	Credit Cards	Subtotal
										-
1/10/2019	2032	ABC Credit								-
										-
										-
										-
										-
										-
										-
										-
										-
										-
										-
										-
										-
										-
										-
Expense Total			-	-	-	-	-	-	-	-

			Health & Fitness	Insurance	Children	Personal	Pets	Travel	Other	Subtotal
Budget				210						**210**
% Spent			-	47.6%	-	-	-	-	-	**47.6%**
Remaining			-	110	-	-	-	-	-	110

Date	Payment Type	Description	Health & Fitness	Insurance	Children	Personal	Pets	Travel	Other	Subtotal
1/1/2019	CrCard	XYZ Supply Store								-
2/5/2019				100.00						100.00
										-
										-
										-
										-
										-
										-
										-
										-
										-
										-
										-
										-
										-
										-
										-
										-
										-
										-
										-
										-
										-
										-
										-
Expense Total			-	-	100.00	-	-	-	-	-	100.00

Envelope System: Another effective method for getting your household budget in order is the envelope system. Please see the website https://www.wikihow.com/Do-Envelope-Budgeting Free!

Another friend recommended "You Need a Budget" at www.youneedabudget.com. It has great reviews; however, this app has a subscription fee to access many of its features.

Let's look at how much the average American spends on LIFE. We use this information to show **you** what the average American spends in specific categories to compare it to your situation. I listed the categories in the same order as in the budget. Use this section to help you clarify the purpose of each category. The numbers that I put into the completed sample budget above come from the information I gathered in the following categories.

Category A: Donations and Gifts

Putting donations and gifts first in the budget may confuse you. "It is my opinion" that you learn financial maturity and wisdom by supporting a charity and its mission. You can embrace the habit of being involved in a "Mission" bigger than yourself.

According to a Motley Fool article written by Selena Maranjian, the average annual household contributed $2,081 to charitable organizations. If you are in difficult financial circumstances, then this category should be zero percent until you make your financial recovery.

According to the National Retail Federation and a Gallup Poll in 2018, Americans will spend about $885 on Christmas gifts! That amount is more than many of those same Americans saved! WOW! Again, according to the National Retail Federation, Americans spent a record $16 billion on Father's Day or $139 per person. Mother's Day earned $25 billion or $195 per person. Men spend more money on both holidays. All I can say is "Keep It Real" if you are on a tight budget. Certainly, never go into debt to keep up with mega consumers.

Category B: Savings and Investment

https://fred.stlouisfed.org/series/PSAVERT

Just as important as giving to a charity, after you balance your budget, your second most important item is to pay yourself. According to the St. Louis Federal Reserve, the average savings rate from the first quarter of 2019 hovered between 6% and 7% of disposable income. Based upon the Real Median Household Income in the U.S. of $60,336 as of 2017, this produces a savings amount of $3921.84 per year. Assorted financial advisors suggest that by your 50's you should have accumulated savings seven times your earnings to meet the financial final exam called "retirement." Unfortunately, many Americans don't pass the test. If you earn $50,000 that equates to $350,000. The *median* savings amount for households between fifty and fifty-five is about $8,000. *Average* savings balance for the same age group is about $124,831. This number is so much higher because of the uber wealthy. The median is more accurate.

According to Value Penguin, in 2016 the Median Savings Balance was $7,000. The average savings balance was $30,600 for the average household, according to the 2016 Survey of Consumer Finances. How do you stack up? If you have more debt than you should, pause saving until your debt is back under control. It makes no sense to collect, say, 5% in a savings vehicle to turn around to pay out 18% in credit card debt interest.

Category C: Home

According to www.apartmentlist.com, the national median price for a one-bedroom apartment is $959 and $1,190 for a 2-bedroom apartment. According to the BLS, the average household spent $11,895 for shelter. The average American mortgage payment according to the U.S. Census Bureau American Housing Survey is $1,030.

According to Zillow, the median value of a home in the U.S. is $227,700. This is where I got the numbers to place in the sample budget above.

Be careful to not overspend in this category. It is easy to justify spending more here because this is the roof over your head. A ballpark figure is to spend one week's salary on your total housing expense. If you make $15.00 per hour and you cannot find safe housing for $600 per month, then consider a responsible roommate.

Category D: Utilities

National average utility cost: https://www.move.org/which-states-pay-most-utilities/

Utility	National Average Cost Per Month
Electricity	$125.22
Natural gas	$100.53
Internet (60 Mbps)	$62.33
Cable	$100
Water	$40
Total Cost of Utilities	$422.08

Here is a table showing average American utility bills. Over several years, I have upgraded my HVAC system, replaced my roof, installed upgraded windows, upgraded appliances and my hot water heater to lower my utility bills. I used AskTrim (https://www.asktrim.com/) to reduce my Direct TV Internet and TV service and then took advantage of employer corporate discounts for cell phone service.

There are a lot of options for mobile cell phone plans. At the time of writing AT&T's prepaid plan, Cricket, Mint Mobile, Verizon prepaid, and Straight Talk offered some of the best cell phone deals. AAA offers deals with Affinity Cellular. Metro by T-Mobile has attractive plans that connect with Amazon Prime. Consumer Cellular offers discount plans to AARP members. Total Wireless uses Verizon's network and is a favorite.

Category E: Food

In the food category, the Bureau of Labor Statistics, American households spend $7,729 per year. They spent $4,363 for food at home and spent $3,365 for food away from home. A great tip for families of four or larger is to invest in a Warehouse Club membership like Costco or BJ's. You will gain a big budget advantage if you buy items in bulk. It saves money! Another big money saver is finding different essential items at Amazon.com, specifically the Amazon Basics brand. I have found a variety of commonly used items, for example, batteries, that are economical.

Category F: Transportation

According to the Bureau of Labor Statistics, the average American household spent $9,576 on transportation expenses in 2017. This includes car payments, car repairs, maintenance, insurance, and gas. This category is a real budget buster. Remember, only about 24% of millionaires drive new cars. Only own the least expensive car that meets your needs. Consider paying 20% of your annual income to purchase a vehicle. That's the thinking that builds wealth and reduces unnecessary debt.

Category G: Credit Cards

This book has an entire chapter (Chapter One) on credit card debt, so I'll be brief here. According to NerdWallet, the "average" revolving credit card debt owed by the "average" U.S. household is $6,741, for $423.8 billion total. The average American household has 2.5 persons. On the surface, this does not look bad. I suspect a small sample of individuals hold most of the debt. Nine percent of Americans feel they can never pay off their credit card debt. The total amount of debt owed by the average American household, including transacting and revolving credit card debt and mortgages, was $135,065 in 2018.

Your goal is **$0.00,** and that is why the guideline is zero percent.

Category H: Health and Fitness

A 2014 Bureau of Labor Statistics chart shows that the average U.S. household spends $4,300 on healthcare and fitness-related expense. This category can include gym memberships, insurance deductibles related to healthcare, and dental expenses. Only pay for the least expensive gym membership you can find. See Chapter Nine: Non-essential Expenses for a more detailed discussion on this topic.

Category I: Insurance

- According to the 2016 data from the Bureau of Labor Statistics, health insurance costs per person are 7.6% of total compensation.

- According to The Zebra, an auto insurance comparison site, the average American spends about $1,500 per year, or about $751 per six-month policy on car insurance.

- The average cost of homeowner's insurance, based upon my calculation of taking each state average from insurance.com, is $1,228 per year. Florida and Louisiana are the most expensive states for homeowner's insurance. Florida's AVERAGE is $3,575. Louisiana's average is $2,979. The average cost of renter's insurance in Florida is lower at $300.

- According to Insurance.com, the average non-smoking forty-year-old American pays $578 annually for a $250,000 term life insurance policy. Smokers pay an average of $1,363 for their life insurance premium. A $50,000 whole life policy for a smoker costs $68 per month for a forty-year-old.

https://www.fool.com/slideshow/heres-what-average-american-spends-these-25-essentials/?slide=25

Category J: Children / Child Care

In these modern times, Child Care is expensive. The Economic Policy Institute website describes daycare expenses by state: https://www.epi.org/child-care-costs-in-the-united-states/

In Florida, the average cost of infant care is $9,238, which amounts to over 17% of the median income of a Florida family. The normal percentage as a part of a family's income is 7%. Keeping childcare expenses below 10% is the best. The survey shows childcare for two children, a baby and a four-year old costs $16,520 per year, or 19.9% more than the average rent in Florida. That's about $1,300 per month.

If you are considering daycare for your children, weigh and calculate alternatives. There are no shortcuts here. Consider a trusted family member to provide daycare. Some workplaces provide daycare facilities for their employees. Check with a nearby school to see if they have an onsite daycare. In my area, it was possible to find an elderly couple, who loved babies and children, who were looking for a little something to do during the week. This type of daycare is less expensive than traditional daycare.

Category K: Personal Care/ Clothes

According to the Bureau of Labor Statistics, the average household spends $1,833 per year on clothes. That's $150 per month. At an outlet store, I get my new clothes off of the clearance rack. I shop at consignment shops. Here is an opportunity to get name brand, gently used clothes at a tremendous discount.

Americans love a good hairdo! They spend $762 per year. Look for hair care coupons, folks. Buy your own razor. Please keep this under control. Sources state that women spend $80 per month and eleven hours a month on that hairdo! Florida has the longest time blow-drying hair at forty-five minutes. Who knew! It adds up to $55,000 in a lifetime, just for hair products and treatments! That's a lot of dough to invest. Look, I like a nice hairdo as much as anybody, but you need to be aware of the total cost of that "do."

Category L: Pets

Pets have become a real obsession in the U.S. Pets are very expensive to own. They can become budget busters. A blog post on www.opploans.com tabulated the average monthly expense per kind of pet.

Here's a breakdown of the data per animal:

- **Birds:** $113.89/month

- **Cats:** $92.98/month

- **Dogs:** $139.80/month

- **Fish:** $62.53/month

- **Mice or Rats:** $80/month

- **Rabbits:** $65/month

- **Reptiles or Turtles:** $116.63/month

- **Small mammals:** $251.82/month

I have two fish and I spend nowhere close to these estimates. Reduce your spending in the pet category. I'll say it again. The market and its nonstop bombardment of advertising shames us into believing we must buy fancy food and take our pets to a fancy pet spa. Not true. Be careful of your local veterinarian going corporate and pressing you to follow through on their expensive "treatment plan." If there is a serious problem, make sure you get a second opinion. Like the auto repair business personnel, veterinarians take sales training classes to learn how to upsell.

Category M: Travel

- According to Valuepenguin.com, average vacation costs (including lodging, food, entertainment, and transportation) for a four-night domestic trip were $581, or $144 per day, and a twelve-day International Trip averaged $3,251, or $271 per day.

- According to Allianz Partner's Vacation Confidence Index in 2019 (the organization sells very profitable travel insurance), Americans expected to spend on vacations this summer an average of $2,037 for a record setting $101.7 billion in 2019. This tops $2,000 for the first time since 2010, when the survey started tracking spending and marking a 5.2% increase over last year. I suspect that post-pandemic spending will be higher now than 2019 because of pent up demand.

- According to the 2017 LearnVest Money Habits and Confessions Survey, 74% of Americans have gone into debt to pay for vacations. The average debt Americans racked up is $1,108. **The survey concluded that 55% of Americans don't (Forgot) put vacation spending in their budget.** https://sctelco.com/learnvest-survey-american-vacation-spending-habits/

- The same survey found that 66% of Americans spent more on their vacations than on one mortgage or rent payment.

- According to Acorn's 2017 Money Matters Report, survey of over 3,000 Americans between eighteen and forty-four, 37% of respondents spent more on vacations than they invested, spending an average of $1,145/year on vacations.

Stealthy Expenses that were not included in the budget

Not listed in the above budget are bank overdraft and late fees. I don't pay them. Part of managing money well is to research the best bank account for your financial situation and never paying bank fees. Sources report bank fees average about $300 per year. Do your best to avoid these fees.

Here is a table from the Bureau of Labor and Statistics on Consumer Expenditures from 2017. Here you can get a ballpark estimate of the percentages each category should/may have.

Table A. Average expenditures and income of all consumer units, 2015-17

| | | | | Percent change | |
Item	2015	2016	2017	2015-16	2016-17
Average income before taxes	$69,627	$74,664	$73,573	7.2	-1.5
Average annual expenditures	55,978	57,311	60,060	2.4	4.8
Food	7,023	7,203	7,729	2.6	7.3
Food at home	4,015	4,049	4,363	0.8	7.8
Food away from home	3,008	3,154	3,365	4.9	6.7
Housing	18,409	18,886	19,884	2.6	5.3
Shelter	10,742	11,128	11,895	3.6	6.9
Owned dwellings	6,210	6,295	6,947	1.4	10.4
Rented dwellings	3,802	4,035	4,167	6.1	3.3
Apparel and services	1,846	1,803	1,833	-2.3	1.7
Transportation	9,503	9,049	9,576	-4.8	5.8
Vehicle purchases	3,997	3,634	4,054	-9.1	11.6
Gasoline, other fuels, and motor oil	2,090	1,909	1,968	-8.7	3.1
Healthcare	4,342	4,612	4,928	6.2	6.9
Health insurance	2,977	3,160	3,414	6.1	8.0
Entertainment	2,842	2,913	3,203	2.5	10.0
Personal care products and services	683	707	762	3.5	7.8
Education	1,315	1,329	1,491	1.1	12.2
Cash contributions	1,819	2,081	1,873	14.4	-10.0
Personal insurance and pensions	6,349	6,831	6,771	7.6	-0.9
Pensions and Social Security	6,016	6,509	6,353	8.2	-2.4
All other expenditures	1,847	1,897	2,010	2.7	6.0

Note: Subcategories do not sum to their respective major item category.

How do you compare?

Time to Improve Your Balance

The Balance Sheet is very important as it determines your net worth. In the United States, about 50% of Americans have a negative net worth.

WalletWise Balance Sheet	Insert Your Figures	LIABILITIES	WalletWise Balance Sheet	Insert Your Figures
Assets			**Liabilities**	
Monetary Assets			**Short Term Liabilities**	
Cash	2.00		Credit Card #1	1.00
Checking Account #1	0.00		Credit Card #2	0.00
Checking Account #2	0.00		Credit Card #3	0.00
Savings Account #1	0.00		Credit Card #4	0.00
Savings Account #2	0.00		Medical Debts	0.00
Savings Account #3	0.00		Past Due Utilities	0.00
Cert. Of Deposit #1	0.00		Past Due Rent	0.00
Cert. Of Deposit #2	0.00		Personal Loans	0.00
Money Market Acc't	0.00		Other	0.00
Other			Other	
Other	0.00		Other	0.00
Total Monetary Assets	2.00		Total Short Term Liabilities	1.00
Tangible Assets			**Long-term Liabilities**	
Vehicle #1	0.00		Vehicle Loan #1	0.00
Vehicle #2	0.00		Vehicle Loan #2	0.00
Home #1	0.00		Home Mortgage #1	1.00
Home #2	0.00		Home Mortgage #2	0.00
Clothing	0.00		Student Loan(s)	0.00
Furniture	0.00		Furniture Loans	0.00
Entertainment Electronics	0.00		Computer Loans	0.00
Home Appliances & Equip.	0.00		Home Appliance Loans	0.00
Computer Equipment	0.00		Personal Loans	0.00
Computer Software	0.00		Other	0.00
Jewelry	0.00		Other	0.00
Recreation Items	0.00		Total Long-term Liabilities	1.00
Personal Property	0.00		TOTAL LIABILITIES	2.00
Other Tangible Assets	0.00			
Total Tangible Assets	0.00			
Investment Assets				
Stocks	0.00			
Bonds	0.00			
Mutual Fund #1	0.00			
Mutual Fund #2	0.00			
Employer Retirement Account(s)	0.00			
IRA Accounts	0.00			
Life Ins. Cash Value(s)	0.00			
Real Estate Investments	0.00			
Collectibles	0.00			
Other Investment Assets	0.00			
Total Investment Assets	0.00			
TOTAL ASSETS	2.00		NET WORTH	0.00

You may spend a lot more than your monthly income, but if your assets are greater than your liability (debt), then you may have a positive net worth.

Balancing Your Checkbook

Speaking of Balance, do you balance your checkbook monthly? The word on the street is not so much. No wonder we do not have a handle on our finances. I learned how to wash a car from someone who was a chauffeur in the 1930s. The reason to hand wash a car in a time without automatic car washes was to get to know your vehicle intimately. You will find the little dents and minor scratches that need touching up. You will notice cuts in the tires. You will see wheel abrasions. The same is true when you balance your checkbook. You will become very intimate with your personal money. You will see where all of it goes. It is essential to balance your checkbook.

Checkbook Statistics

Why should you balance your checkbook? Because, you can check for bank errors and theft. That's right. I noticed my balance (which was razor thin) went negative (I was overdrawn) and I incurred an overdraft fee. I looked at my statement (before online apps) and noticed a charge that neither my wife nor I had started. With a little research discovered that a local photographer had gotten the card number to my wife's debit card and charged the card for a bogus transaction. I immediately marched down to my local bank branch and demanded the return of the stolen money and the overdraft fee. If I did not have a handle on my checking account, I would never have known about the fraud. You can balance your checkbook. It takes fifteen minutes.

Here is how I do it. You will need your checkbook ledger, your latest bank statement, a calculator, pencil, and a highlighter.

If you are not recording every transaction in your checkbook ledger, then it is time you begin. Some folks say they don't use checks much anymore and only use their debit card and/or pay everything online with a credit card. Inaccurate expense tracking may result. In my financial coaching business, I ask for checking and credit card statements on paper to create the budget. To balance your checkbook, we only need to see the expenses you are paying with the debit card associated with your checking account, checks you write out of your checking account, and cash withdrawals you make from your checking account. If you try this exercise and are having difficulty, go to your bank branch in person and ask an associate to assist you in balancing your checkbook.

Here we go!

I match my checking account statement transactions, starting with deposits and moving to withdrawals to my checkbook ledger. I put a tick mark by the item on the statement and the ledger to show I have recorded all transactions properly in the ledger. If you have a lot of ATM withdrawals, they need to be posted in the ledger, otherwise balancing your checkbook gets difficult. In fact, your checkbook ledger is an excellent tool to track expenses. After you have made sure your ledger numbers look identical to your statement, you are now ready to fill out the reconciliation form to see if everything balances. First, fill in the spot where outstanding (unpaid checks go). This is very important. These are items you have subtracted from your balance in your ledger, but the bank has not paid and has not subtracted from your balance (therefore, you appear to have more money in your account than you really do). Remove this discrepancy by recording these unpaid items. Locate the bank's account statement ending balance and then subtract the unpaid outstanding items. The result should match your checkbook ledger amount. If it does not, go back to the beginning and recheck your addition and subtraction of the deposits and withdrawals in your ledger. Recheck you're the addition of the outstanding checks. Make sure what you wrote in your ledger matches the bank statement. Do this until both the bank account statement and your checkbook ledger match.

Sample Check Ledger

Codes - **ACH**: ACH Payment | **ATM**: Cash Withdrawal | **BP**: Bill Payment | **DC**: Debit Card | **D**: Deposit | **DD**: Direct Deposit | **SF**: Service Fee | **WT**: Wire Transfer						
CHECK NUMBER/ CODE	**DATE**	**TRANSACTION DESCRIPTION**	**(–) PAYMENT/ DEBIT**	**✓**	**(+) DEPOSIT/ CREDIT**	**BALANCE**
		Starting Balance				

Sample Checking Account Reconciliation Form

CHECKING ACCOUNT RECONCILIATION FORM

JUST ANSWER THE FOLLOWING QUESTIONS TO "BALANCE YOUR CHECKBOOK".

1. What is the amount shown on this statement for ENDING BALANCE? $ _______________

2. Have you made any deposits that have not been credited on this statement? Total up these deposits and enter the amount.   + $ _______________

3. ADD TOGETHER Lines 1 and 2.   = $ _______________

4. Are there any outstanding checks, payments, transfers or other withdrawals that are not reflected on this statement? Use the table below to add them up and enter the total on the left.   - $ _______________

5. Subtract Line 4 from Line 3. This should reflect your checkbook balance.   = $ _______________

LIST CHECKS OUTSTANDING NOT CHARGED TO YOUR CHECKING ACCOUNT					
Check Number	Amount	Check Number	Amount	Check Number	Amount
				Enter in Line 4	TOTAL ▶

IF YOU DO NOT BALANCE 1. Verify additions and subtractions above and in your check register; 2. Compare the dollar amounts of checks listed on this statement with the check amounts listed in our check register; 3. Compare the dollar amounts of deposits listed on this statement with the deposit amounts recorded in your check register.

Sample Check

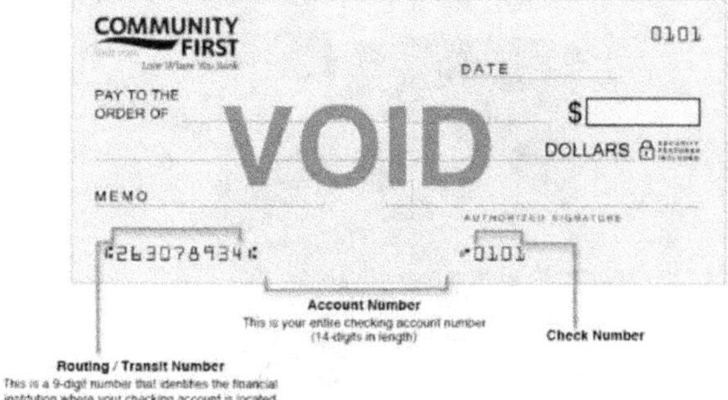

Other Important Tips

1. Make sure you record automatic deposits and withdrawals in your ledger immediately. It helps keep the records in chronological order and makes balancing your checkbook easier.

2. Record other transactions in your checkbook ledger daily. Waiting a week to record a stack of receipts can lead to errors. When you write a check, you ought to have the ledger with you.

3. Record debit transactions.

4. Log on and check your online checking account entries with your ledger recordings to make sure everything is consistent.

5. Don't forget to subtract fees: ATM fees, check refill fees, etc.

https://www.thebalance.com/how-to-keep-a-running-balance-of-your-account-2385978

Motivate yourself to complete this project by indulging in a reward afterward!

After you have successfully balanced your checkbook, indulge yourself in a reward. It could just be a piece of chocolate—doesn't have to be a whole banana split. Plus, banana splits are expensive in more ways than one.

Automation

Luckily, we live in a connected, technical world that I could not have imagined when I started in the business world. It's easier than ever before to keep track of your money using a digital smartphone application. My go-to budgeting app is MINT. The company that sells TurboTax, Quicken, and QuickBooks developed the MINT app. It connects to all of your bank accounts and keeps a running balance for you. Program the application to send you notices triggered by important events, like, you have run out of money. Stop spending! No, seriously, it's like another set of eyes. There are other budget applications out there, but MINT works; it's really free, and it does not upsell you anything.

Another popular app is Truebill, https://www.truebill.com/. It is a great app, but costs about $40.00 per year. Its claim to fame is to assist you in keeping track of unwanted digital subscriptions. Most credit card apps will take you to a page that shows your digital subscriptions. Another method to fight unneeded subscriptions is to report fraud on your credit card. It usually happens to me organically about twice a year. The credit card company sends you a new card with a new number and expiration date. Then, wait, you will start receiving emails from all of your subscription services asking you to update your credit card payment information. If you think I'm a rascal for using this technique, that's fine. I call it taking back control of your finances. Renew only the necessary subscriptions.

Online Banking

You will use your computer and your cellphone to access your bank in this era of online banking. You can make deposits using an app on your phone, download statements, check your balance, transfer money between accounts, and pay bills. You can tell (ask) your boss to deposit your paycheck directly into your account. Most employers are on board here because it is easier for them. With online banking, it is easy to set up automatic savings and pay yourself first. With online bill pay, you can pay your credit card bills, utility bills, insurance bills without having to write a check, address an envelope or buy a stamp, etc. Online banking allows you to set up message alerts that inform you of any account activity. You can adjust the settings of the alerts so you just hear about the big stuff. Online banking allows you to download and print your statements to use for balancing your checkbook with pencil and paper.

I recently surfed my online banking portal and found a Spending & Budgeting tool. However, it is not as efficient and effective as budgeting with paper and pencil. Why should you use pencil and paper you might ask? The online application is not as specific as our above pen and paper budget. There is something different about your focus on balancing a checkbook or creating a budget by using pencil and paper versus a digital tool. Changes can be made faster than on a computer. You do not have to have an internet connection (get your statement mailed to you) and you can eliminate most (turn your phone off) electronic distractions.

What is Zelle? With apps like Zelle, you can repay friends person to person for money owed, pay your part of a restaurant tab, or repay someone for a concert ticket they bought you. You can do similar activities by tapping phones (tap & pay) with the right apps. In fact, mobile phones have themselves become mobile banks. Bank apps on your phone (Citi Card, Apple Pay, Google Pay) create digital wallets that store your credit card information to allow you to pay at participating vendors.

Education

Use the resources available on my website, https://www.walletwise.org/downloadableresources.

Check out www.cashcourse.org. It allows you to sign up for additional financial skill lessons and courses. Student accounts are free.

Chapter 4

Money Management and Budgeting

Summary Questions

Exercise Time: *approximately 25 minutes*

I.   *Is ignorance of personal finances a good idea? Why not?*

II.   *On a scale of 1-10, how practical have you found "the six steps plan" to be?*

III.   *Do you think budgeting is a tool to restrict you or an exercise to help you organize your finances?*

IV.   *What will you do if your expenses exceed your income? Also, state your reasons?*

      a. Ask for a raise?

      b. Begin a Side Hustle?

      c. Would you consider reducing expenses?

V.   *List several practical ways to know if you are spending more than you make without a Budget.*

VI.   *Do you balance your checkbook monthly? Why is it important?*

VII.   *Why is net worth important to calculate? How would you convince someone to calculate theirs? Would a bank calculate this if you apply for a mortgage?*

VIII.   *What does it mean if you have a negative net worth?*

A Few Interesting Tasks

1. Download the digital version of the WalletWise Budget, open it in Excel and begin the journey of creating your budget. Print it out and fill it in to get a novel experience of working with pencil and paper.

2. Download the Expense Tracker and print it. Carry it with you until your spending habits are clear to you.

3. Download the Net Worth Worksheet and calculate your net worth. This is a no judgement zone.

Chapter 5

Know Your Credit Score and Understand Your Credit Report

"I have always advocated doing everything possible to pay off credit

card balances; it's good financial management and the ticket to a

strong FICO credit score"

—Suze Orman

First things first! Everyone in the United States that has ever borrowed money in any form or simply rented an apartment has a credit report assigned to their identity. Good personal money management is an important skill for you to learn because bad money management results in a lower personal credit score for you. If you score low on this "special" type of report card, you will pay higher interest rates on your debts. Lower credit scores often lead consumers to do business with unscrupulous or predatory lenders. Please remember The Big Three Credit Bureaus do not work for you, and they may treat you as an inconvenience! The credit bureaus work for the lenders! They do not care if their records about you are incorrect, if your address is incorrect, or they incorrectly marked your credit with a negative rating. They have no incentive to keep your records correct. A negative report justifies the lender charging you more for a loan than if the report was correct, so there is little motivation for them to correct their mistakes. You decide if that is a conflict of interest. Credit bureaus collect credit information and credit scores and then resell your information for a fee to lenders, employers, and insurance companies. Utilities, cable TV, internet and cell phone companies are interested in your credit report. That's the purpose of the credit bureaus. They sell your data to these companies. The companies buying your data are the customers. Credit bureaus are not in the business of helping you correct the data of the credit consumers. Monitor the information and correct any incorrect information yourself. A good credit score can help you get out of poverty and move into the middle class. It directly affects how much interest you pay on a mortgage. I dislike debt, but debt to build wealth if you were not born *ballin* (Well-to-Do) is okay.

Understanding Credit Repair

The Fair Credit Reporting Act gives you the right to correct errors, but you have to do the work.

You can do this! Updating your records, disputing errors, and monitoring your credit report is important. Your reward for doing this work is an accurate credit report which will result in you saving money on your **debt!** The Internet has made these chores easier for you.

Bad credit can stay on your report for up to seven years. So, putting yourself in a bad credit situation makes your life more difficult and expensive. There is good news, though. By monitoring your credit reports regularly, you can dispute legitimate errors in reporting of late or missed payments. The credit bureau will have to respond within thirty days, updating your report. If they do not, rerun your report and file another dispute until they get it right. As I mentioned earlier, credit bureaus work for the lenders. Ask your lenders who are reporting late payments in error to report your payments on time.

Shhhh. A little nugget: if you are making a major purchase, Such as a house or car, your lender may have the power to contact the credit bureau and remove questionable negative files, so you and your lender can move forward with the transaction.

Do Not Hire A Credit Recovery Company!

Credit repair companies cannot do anything you can't do yourself. Remember, the credit bureau can remove only inaccurate information from your credit report. By law, the three major credit bureaus must correct errors in your report. The three major credit bureaus have instructions for correcting mistakes in your report.

1. www.experian.com

2. www.transunion.com

3. www.equifax.com

What's in the Report?

The credit report is a report card of your credit accounts. Each bureau has a different format, but every report has a list of your open credit accounts, the name of the creditor, the amount borrowed, date of last payment received, length of account, and a listing of any missed or late payments. Credit card lenders, your mortgage, car loans, student loans, and other unsecured creditors submit the information to your report. Reports can include public record filings like liens, foreclosures, bankruptcies, court judgments, and civil suits. The reports include any recent applications or inquiries you made for credit. Credit reports keep a detailed description of your personal information. This information includes your current and former addresses, birthdate, Social Security number, and phone numbers.

Order Your Free Credit Report:

It is important that you monitor your credit by ordering a free copy of your report. The credit bureaus allow you to receive one free copy of their reports once a year.

Get your credit report free once per year from this site:

https://www.annualcreditreport.com/index.action

Make sure you are on the correct site because there are many companies offering free credit reports. However, many are imposters.

If you Google **free credit report**, "annual credit report.com" is fifth on the list. The first searches result in legitimate companies offering free credit reports or FICO scores, but they will try to sell you something (credit monitoring and identity theft products you do not need, etc.) during your time on their site. "Annualcreditreport.com" will allow you to set up one account to access all three credit bureaus. It is wise to ask for one report from one bureau every four months so you can monitor throughout the year at no charge. If a major company or your credit bureau has a large data breach, they may entitle you to a free credit monitoring for at least one year as part of the breach settlement. The three credit bureaus are Experian, TransUnion, and Equifax.

Fun Fact: 57% of consumers checked at least one of their credit reports in 2018. You should, too!

Credit Scores and FICO

Besides your credit report, when you apply for credit, lenders pay the credit bureaus for your credit score. Complex computer formulas managed by a corporation called Fair Isaac Corporation calculate your FICO score and also analyze your credit report history data. www.fico.com.

The banking industry introduced the FICO score in 1989. In the 50s, Bill Fair and Earl Isaac created an automated scoring system that sadly flopped. It took thirty years for the scoring system to evolve into an acceptable credit scoring system to the banking industry. That is how the Fair, Isaac, and Company was born.

FICO scores and use numerical ratings to grade your credit worthiness. Lenders use 27 million

FICO scores every day and use FICO scores in over 90% of lending decisions.

Here is a link to a great video describing FICO scores:

https://youtu.be/OwIlRGsqxUg

Here is a link to my FICO that shows the interest increase required based on different credit

scores. https://www.myfico.com/credit-education/calculators/loan-savings-calculator/

A good "rule of thumb" of credit score ranges

300-629	Bad
630-689	Fair
690-719	Good
720-850	Excellent

Credit bureaus use the following ingredients to grade your credit and create your credit score:

1. Payment History
   a. Payment History accounts for about 35% of your total credit score and is considered the most important aspect of your credit history.
   b. The easiest way to improve your credit score is to make all of your payments on time.

2. Credit Utilization

    a. How much credit of your "available" credit are you using? If you max out your credit lines, you have no wiggle room or margin.

    b. Borrowers with the best scores use only 6% of their available credit.

    c. This is another reason to be careful closing unused credit accounts too quickly. Closing an old, unused credit account reduces your utilization ratio and lowers your credit score. Sometimes what seems right (closing an account) is not.

    d. Credit Utilization accounts for about 30% of your score.

3. Length of Credit History

    a. Communicates to lenders your history of borrowing.

    b. Accounts for only 15% of your score.

4. New Credit

    a. Only apply for credit when absolutely necessary.

    b. Multiple credit inquiries tell lenders you may be in credit stress and looking to borrow from a new account to pay off another debt.

    c. Be careful. A "hard" credit inquiry on your credit report is reported and affects your credit score.

    d. A "soft" inquiry means they checked your credit without it being reported or affecting your score.

    e. When you are shopping for new credit or looking at preapproval credit offers, demand a soft inquiry until you are serious about applying for credit.

    f. New Credit inquiries account for only 10% of your score.

g. When making a major purchase like a home or car, shop for different credit with different lenders in a brief burst of time, so that the credit bureaus merge multiple hard inquiries into one reported hard inquiry.

5. Credit Mix

a. A vague category that shows a variety of credit history.

b. Credit Mix accounts for only 10% of your score.

A good FICO score is 720. 760 is better. This is a wonderful goal. Good credit scores make it easier for you to borrow money, get credit cards with better interest rates and benefits, and have better cell phone plans and insurance premiums. Many employers will check your credit. Why? Employers do not want employees receiving stressful debt collection calls at work. They don't want stressed out and distracted employees. Insurance companies check your credit file. Insurance companies know that stressed out, debt-ridden drivers are statistically more prone to get into an accident, causing an expensive claim. Ain't debt fun?

However, you get to decide who has access to your credit report. All interested parties must have your permission to look at your credit file.

Did you know you have an Insurance Risk Score?

You can get your insurance score! Your insurance score is like a credit score, but is specific score to rating your insurance risk to insurance companies. Check out personalreports.lexisnexis.com to get your auto and home insurance reports.

Check out this Loan Savings Calculator. I included this calculator here to show you how your credit score affects the interest rate you qualify for. A 620-639 low-score borrower gets charged

4.9% while the 760-850 borrower gets charged 3.35% interest. Over a 30-year mortgage loan, that adds up to a lot of money.

https://www.myfico.com/credit-education/calculators/loan-savings-calculator/

Many credit card companies (Discover, Citi) offer free FICO scores. In fact, FICO lists 170 partners in their FICO Score Open Access Program that allow you access to your score. Just make sure their partner does not charge you for your credit score.

Here is what a FICO credit score looks like.

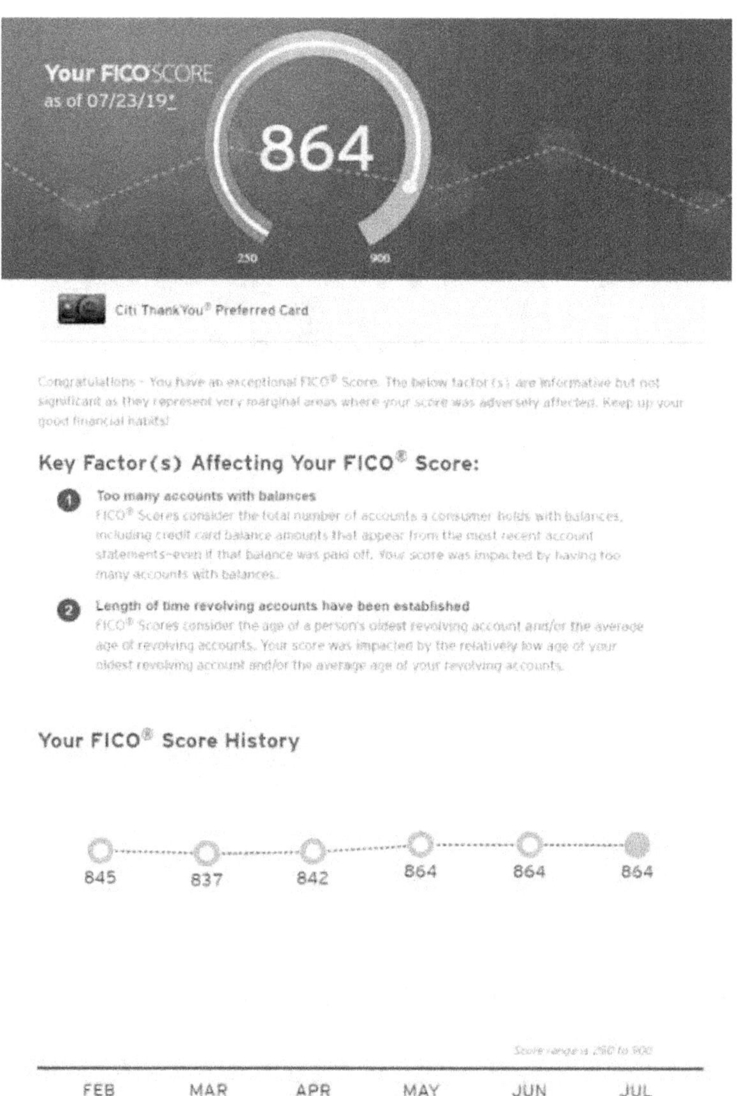

To ensure your Credit Score is High, do the following:

- Pay bills on time.

- Pay off debt instead of moving it to a new consolidation account.

- If you have missed payments, get current and stay current.

- Avoid having payments go to collection agencies.

- Keep outstanding balances low on credit cards.

- Don't close unused accounts.

- Shop for the best rates.

- Do not allow anyone (INCLUDING YOUR CHILDREN) to use your credit card.

- Check your own credit reports and FICO score every year. Checking your own credit report or FICO score does not lower your FICO score.

Try using a credit monitoring app (that may come free with your bank or credit card company) that allows you to check your credit score at no charge. This is a great resource if you use credit responsibly. It will compare offers to aid you in getting the best credit product for you. Try https://www.creditkarma.com/, to monitor your credit score.

In the spirit of keeping your credit score as high as possible, the following discussion helps you control access to your credit report and protect yourself from identity thieves. Identity theft can begin by someone accessing your credit report illegally. Debt accounts opened in your name can negatively affect your credit score. Here are a few ideas to prevent that:

Credit Freeze

A credit freeze is a security lock on your credit reports to prevent someone from opening an account in your name. This prevents identity theft and the consumer credit bureaus from selling and reselling your credit information encouraging credit providers to send tempting credit offers to you every day in the mail. That's right, besides selling your credit data for legitimate inquiries by apartment complexes, lenders, insurance companies and employers, the credit bureaus equally sell your data to prospective lenders who use it to market unsolicited credit- based products to you.

Inform each credit bureau separately to apply the freeze. Credit freeze services are free and mandated by federal law. Credit freezes legally protect you from loss.

Do not confuse a credit freeze with a credit lock. They are two different things. Credit locks are not free, but they and credit freezes both protect your credit files. Companies like Credit Karma and LifeLock usually provide them as part of a paid subscription.

Stay with the Freeze.

Equifax

Equifax.com/personal/credit-report-services

800-349-9960

Experian

https://www.experian.com/freeze/center.html

888-EXPERIAN (888-397-3742)

They will each provide you a PIN that is a "must save" to unlock your frozen account. Therefore, it is important for you to protect this PIN. You must have a **reliable method** for saving important documents, passwords, and PIN numbers.

A credit freeze does not affect your credit score. A credit freeze does not prevent you from getting your free, annual credit reports. You can easily unlock your credit freeze when a lender, employer, or insurance company needs to access your files.

You can also start a Fraud Alert on your credit accounts if you lost your wallet or other personal data. The Fraud Alert lasts one year. There is an extended Fraud Alert for those who have experienced identity theft, and this alert lasts seven years. Please read Chapter One: Credit Cards for a detailed discussion of Identity Theft and Fraud.

Please check out this amazing Federal Trade Commission Website that explains much of this:

https://www.consumer.ftc.gov/articles/0497-credit-freeze-faqs#what

OptOutPrescreen.com

Another way to control the distribution of your data is to use the official opt out choice called OptOutPrescreen.com. https://www.optoutprescreen.com

This service is free and allows you to opt out of receiving credit offers for five years. Hallelujah!

For History Buffs: How did Credit Bureaus Start?

Before the era of computers and credit scores, lending in the United States was, well…

interesting. Financially capable entrepreneurs located credit bureaus in each town to provide the

service of checking credit on customers of department stores and banks wanting credit. A credit

bureau employee would call the local department store you listed on your credit application and

ask the owner, "How does Sam pay his bill to ABC Mercantile?" The actual name "Credit

Bureau" identifies a list of people in town that are poor credit risks. Eventually, credit bureaus

merged into larger entities that later became the Big Three Credit Bureaus we have now. Equifax

started in Atlanta as the Retail Credit Company in 1899. In 1975, their name changed to Equifax.

TransUnion started in 1968 as a Tank Car company. In the late sixties, it started acquiring

regional and city credit bureaus. In 1969, TransUnion bragged it stored files on 3.6 million index

cards! Experian started in England in 1980. Experian moved into the US in 1996 with its

acquisition of TRW Information Systems. TRW was the largest credit bureau in the US.

In 1970, Congress passed the Fair Credit Reporting Act (FCRA) to make sure consumers' credit

files were correct.

https://www.consumerfinance.gov/learnmore/

This act is the federal law that allows you to dispute and correct errors, ask for a credit score, and

put or remove a security freeze on your credit history. This is the law that permits you to get a

free annual copy of your report from each of the Big Three.

Conclusion:

A good credit report and credit score results in lower debt cost for you. A good credit score does

not happen by accident. You must take responsibility for your credit score by making your

payments on time, contacting the credit bureau to fix errors, and monitoring your credit reports annually to make sure your credit report information is as accurate as possible. Your credit score is a "special" report card they do not teach you about in school. This report card, if managed well, can save you thousands of dollars in interest over your lifetime.

Chapter 5

Know Your Credit Score and Understand Your Credit Report

Summary Questions

Exercise Time: *approximately 20 minutes*

The perfect mindset for this exercise is to focus on the results of having a good credit score.

   a.   *How do you find your free credit report?*

   b.   *What's the best way to find your credit score?*

   c.   *What credit behaviors make up a credit score?*

   d.   *What is the difference between a credit freeze and a credit lock?*

   e.   *What are the five main credit report determinants or criteria?*

   f.   *Do you think monitoring your credit report is important?*

   g.   *How many lenders use FICO score every day?*

Task Time

Go to https://www.annualcreditreport.com/index.action open an account and check your score.

Check and see if your credit card bank provides you with a free credit score and locate your score.

Chapter 6

Real Estate

"Owning a home is a keystone of wealth — both financial affluence and emotional security." -
—Suze Orman

What are the actual costs of renting versus owning real estate? This chapter is not a complete discussion of real estate. There are volumes of books out there about real estate. This chapter discusses the purchase and sale of real estate and the financial aspects of renting. Use this chapter as a guideline to make smart decisions about renting and owing real estate. Housing costs are our largest expense, and we require skills and knowledge to make smart choices. I want you to be in a safe, sustainable home. Having a home is the key to less financial and emotional stress.

Source:

1) https://www.cnbc.com/2017/04/07/heres-how-much-more-it-costs-to-own-vs-rent-a-home-in-every-us-state.html

2) https://www.nerdwallet.com/blog/mortgages/cost-homeownership-vs-renting/

Rent or Buy?

Our friends at CNBC say that homeownership is from 35 to 90 percent more expensive than renting. Nerd Wallet says it is 33% to 93% more expensive to purchase than to rent. Researchers base the difference in cost on real estate taxes and maintenance costs from specific locations. Know your state numbers. If you plan to purchase, make sure you can afford all the expenses: taxes, homeowner's insurance, and home maintenance. It appears if you are planning to live in the same area for a period longer than five years, it may make sense to purchase. Home ownership reaps the rewards of financial security, some tax deductions, inflation protection and the opportunity to own a property outright with no mortgage payment. It is important to recognize your home's primary purpose is to provide a roof over your head. Many people think owning real estate is a get rich quick plan. Owning real estate is a foundation to accumulating wealth, but that is not the purpose of your house.

"Don't wait to buy real estate. Buy real estate and wait." -*Will Rogers.*

The major headache of renting a home is not being in control over the cost of rent. You could find yourself priced out of a home if you live in a rising rent location.

Mortgages

Fun Fact. The word mortgage is French. The French define the word mortgage as "death pledge."

Experiment with your budget before you purchase. Estimate your mortgage payment first by researching the prices of homes in the area. Say your mortgage payment will be $1,000 per month (based on a $225,000 purchase price). Save an additional $300 per month or add 30% to your estimated mortgage payment while you are still renting to see how home ownership will affect your pocketbook. The total cost of $1,300 will better reflect the total cost of home ownership.

It's not just about the mortgage cost! Remember that there are real estate taxes, homeowner's insurance, and maintenance costs to consider.

Find a reputable mortgage broker. Locate a professional mortgage broker to get your mortgage pre-approval. Pre-approval can put you in a better negotiating position compared to more experienced negotiators or cash buyers. The mortgage broker must connect you to a competent lender. In a

"HOT" real estate market, they must attach your offer to a lender that can close fast. It's another negotiating point in your favor.

McMansion buyers beware! Buy a smaller house than you can afford. Remember, the Realtor and mortgage broker are in a conflict of interest with you. They want you to buy the **most** house you can afford (according to them, not you) and then borrow the most amount of money they think you can afford. Why? Because the lender receives a commission or additional fees based on production. Therefore, whether or not you can really afford the property isn't their primary concern! Think to buy less than you can afford! The Thomas J. Stanley book, *The Millionaire Next Door,* reports that most millionaires in the United States live in modest homes. The folks that live in the mansions want you to think they are wealthy. They are not. They are just "house poor." In 2014 during the housing recovery in Deland, Florida, it was possible to purchase a modest block three-bedroom house in a safe neighborhood for $50,000—if you had cash.

In 2021, those same houses sell for $250,000. Oh my!

http://clark.com/homes-real-estate/price-rent-headed-down/

Online mortgage applications are popular and 50% of prospective home buyers use them. Seventy-five percent did at least a portion of their application online.

The most popular include:

- Quicken Loans
- Lending Tree
- Better.com
- Rocket Mortgage (a subsidiary of Quicken Loans)
- Chase
- Bank of America, a traditional bank, offers an online component.

Truth in Lending Act

Make sure you read the fine print of your mortgage application. A lot of the chicanery during the Financial Crises was because of shifty clauses in the mortgage applications and the mortgages themselves. Because I owned my business, I ended up with a mortgage with an archaic prepayment penalty. I should have walked out of the closing. I learned about the prepayment penalty at closing and not before. The mortgage broker did not want to take the risk that I would not accept. I should have seen this information in the "Good Faith Estimate," but I did not see it until the closing. It was a time when you shuffled and signed papers but did not read them. The "Good Faith Estimate" discloses and reports the expenses related to your new mortgage. Get it within three days of its preparation. Make sure you understand what you are agreeing to before you get to your closing! Insist on seeing your "Good Faith Estimate"!

Due Diligence

If you are renting or buying, visit lots of locations (fifty is a good start, really!) and ask lots of questions. If you are purchasing, do the research. Check the schools. Check the property taxes. Check criminal activity and if law enforcement is on the ball.

Purchasing a house in an unfamiliar location, right before the 2008 financial crises, was a tough choice to make. Home prices throughout the nation were rising with no end in sight. It seemed if you did not buy now, then you would never get a home. Unregulated lending practices created the perfect setting for a bubble. This happened to a friend of mine who purchased a home that later resulted in foreclosure. He bought an older house that was owned by a house flipper. An investor bought it and fixed it. The house was in a low-lying area near the water. The realtor did not disclose the flood issue to the buyer. Every time it rained the plumbing failed.

Check the house on a rainy day. No kidding. Don't forget to check the basement after a rainstorm. Yup, not everyone lives in Florida (where there are almost no basements).

In fact, if the home you are purchasing has insurance claims, it may be difficult to insure. Check your property's CLUE report at https://personalreports.lexisnexis.com/fact_act_disclosure.jsp.

I'm sure it overjoyed the bank to repossess this gem. My favorite part is that when the house was sold, the real estate agent and the mortgage broker were well compensated and lost nothing in the upcoming result—foreclosure. Be careful purchasing real estate near the waterfront. My house has been the go-to shelter for family members during close calls with hurricanes. Remember, if you buy property on low-lying ground near the water, expect to evacuate. Evacuation is inconvenient.

Consider the Location of Your New Home

Living in Florida, I have seen the devastation incurred by hurricanes. Beach erosion and wind damage turn multimillion dollar properties into splinters. Be careful when you purchase a property. Besides purchasing in a geographically sensitive location, consider traffic patterns, air traffic patterns, and proximity to other nuisances, like:

- Edge of a cliff;

- Next to a racetrack;

- Next to a popular Tourist Attraction;

- On the Beach;

- Near the Beach;

- Next to a Dry Forest;

- At the bottom of a Geographic Bowl;

- Next to an Airport;

- Next to a Military Airbase;

- On the Flight line of an airport or Military Airbase;

- Next to a Railroad Track;

- Across the Street from a Bar;

- Next to an Overcrowded School where cars clog the street twice a day.

If you buy a home in an area that experiences floods, hurricanes, and fires, you need additional expensive insurance to protect against floods, mudslides, or fire.

Yes, buyer beware. And no, insurance companies are not evil. They are just protecting their investment from the risks man and nature create.

Caveat emptor is Latin for "Buyer Beware!"

Don't be shy about visiting your potential new home at a different time of the day. Does that cute school right down the street dismiss at 2:30, which results in cars lining up around the block? Is your new home near train tracks or below a military base flight path?

Make sure there is an accurate survey. If you are financing, this is a requirement. The survey protects the lender, not you. Get a survey specifically for yourself. Rural real estate transactions have special concerns. Make sure legal access "egress and ingress" is described in the title. There is such a thing as being landlocked with no "official" access. Read: very expensive to fix. I've been there, saw that!

Is there a homeowner's association? Almost everything I've heard about them is negative. I've never lived in a neighborhood with one. There are lots of rules, other neighbors in your business, and you still have to pay for this "luxury". Sign me up, NOT!!

The average American household (about 2.5 people) spends about $56,000 to exist, according to the Bureau of Labor Statistics. Out of that, Americans on average spend $18,400 per year, or average $1,500 per month on housing. Divide the $1,500 by 2.5 folks per household and you get about $600 per month per person for housing expenses.

Real Estate Agents

Interview multiple realtors. Hire the right agent! In hot markets, be aware of bidding scams. Beware of agents giving false hope to novice buyers, using their offers to bid up the price of a property and forcing the seasoned deep-pocket-buyer to offer a higher price on the same property. Never believe in verbal promises. Don't waive your right to inspect the property. And yes, pay for your own inspection.

http://clark.com/homes-real-estate/pro-tips-how-to-find-the-best-real-estate-agent-for-you/

Most of the real estate agents out there are professionals, but if you are new to the area, then buyer beware. Hire an experienced agent who is well informed in your area and price range. You may end up with a previously flipped house remodeled by amateurs. The house may be in a low-lying area requiring you to evacuate during a major storm. The Realtor still gets paid their commission, regardless. If you are moving to a new area, rent first, and then consider purchasing. We do not find deals, we make them. Remember to calculate taxes and insurance to determine total payment. Houses always need repairs. Budget for this. Buy something less than you can afford. Replacement roofs, windows, flooring, air conditioning units etc. don't come cheap. Post-pandemic, remodeling and appliance prices have skyrocketed.

Other factors that affect ownership include your age. It may be better to rent when you are younger or if you know in advance that you are staying five years or less to make it easier to move during career transitions requiring relocation. Another factor is stress. It's stressful buying and selling real estate. Are you up for it?

Check out this "Rent vs. Buy" calculator free from Realtor.com.

https://www.nytimes.com/2014/05/22/upshot/rent-or-buy-the-math-is-changing.html

Don't forget about homeowner's insurance. Go for replacement coverage. It will cover the full cost instead of the depreciated cost of the damage.

When purchasing a home through conventional financing, it is best to put 20% down for your down payment. FHA loans only require a 3.5% down payment. FHA loans are more flexible with less than perfect credit borrowers. However, any mortgage, including FHA, requires PMI insurance for any loan to value ratio less than 20%. After your loan to value ratio drops below 78%, you can refinance to drop the PMI. Under a conventional mortgage, you can drop PMI. PMI is Private Mortgage Insurance required on any home loan with less than 20% loan to value. PMI gives mortgage lenders protection in case of foreclosure. Homes with low loan to value ratios foreclose more often. PMI, on average, costs 1% (per month) of loan value. If you are a veteran, you may qualify for a VA mortgage loan. They are 0% down and backed by the US Government, so no PMI. They also have less stringent qualification standards. You will only want a fixed-rate loan. The uncertainty of variable rates was one cause of excessive mortgage defaults causing the financial crises in 2008.

I do this! I pay my real estate taxes and homeowner's insurance. I don't escrow. There is no reason to deposit homeowner's insurance money into your lender's account, earning interest for the bank and not you. Keep control of your money. Just don't forget to budget for these expenses. If you don't pay them, the bank will. That service comes at a high cost to you.

I do this! I pay additional principal each month on my mortgage to pay it off faster and save on interest. I began with a 30-year loan and refinanced it when interest rates came down. I requested to keep the remaining term the same. This means I did not reset the clock to 30 years like many do when they refinance. My remaining term was 24 years, and it was no problem. My payment still went down without extending the term. **DO NOT EXTEND THE TERM!** I considered refinancing with a new 15-year term. These loans have very attractive interest rates because the bank gets their money back so much sooner. Here's my philosophy: if I accept a 15-year term, I cannot in the middle of things change back to 30. Meaning, if I lose my job or have some other unexpected financial hardship (emergency fund) my 24-year payment is less than the 15-year term payment. With a 15-year term, I've locked myself into the higher payment no matter what. With the longer term, I can always pay more when everything is good. I started out paying an extra $50.00 per month, which equated to making one additional payment per year. Yes, I know. My mortgage is inexpensive. That's from refinancing at a lower rate a few times. I may do it again.

Now I pay almost double payments. At the end of 2019, my wife retired (not of her choosing) and if she does not get a new job that pays as well, we will be okay. But not so okay if I had locked myself into the higher payment 15-year loan. Check out:

https://www.daveramsey.com/mortgage-payoff-calculator

https://www.mortgagecalculator.net/early-pay-off/

Make biweekly payments. Instead of 12 monthly payments, pay 26 biweekly payments. Every year you will pay an added month of principal.

If you pay a little extra each month, you will save in the long run. Don't pay your lender to set this service up for you. Do it yourself.

Know how to Read your Mortgage Statement

STATEMENT BREAKDOWN

We'll say it again: Mortgage statements shouldn't require an advanced degree in finance (plus a minor in statistical analysis) to read.

We're constantly listening to your feedback and working to make your statements easier to understand.

Here are the key facts on your monthly statement, with a handy visual guide to finding them:

1. STATEMENT INFORMATION

Here are the basic basics, like the date your statement was generated, loan number, amount due, and your payment due date.

2. EXPLANATION OF AMOUNT DUE

A breakdown of your payment, showing the amount for principal, interest and escrow. If there are optional items, late payments or other fees, they will be shown here as well. Click here to see our complete fee schedule.

3. ACCOUNT OVERVIEW

This will tell you your principal balance, escrow balance, and your current interest rate.

4. PAST PAYMENT BREAKDOWN

This section recaps your last payment and also the payments you've made to date this year. It shows how much went to principal, interest, escrow, optional insurance, and any miscellaneous fees.

5. HELPFUL INFORMATION

Here you'll find important explanations and special notices pertaining to your account, plus useful tips for managing your home loan.

6. TRANSACTION ACTIVITY

A basic recap of your recent transactions on your account and the resulting balances, as well as disbursements we've made on your behalf to payees like tax authorities and insurance providers. Want to see more? Sign in to your account.

7. PAYMENT COUPON

If you pay by mail, please fill out, detach, and return this section with your check or money order. It's easy. But the easiest and fastest way to pay is online. Sign in to your account to make a one-time payment or set-up AutoPay. It's free and you never have to lick a stamp.

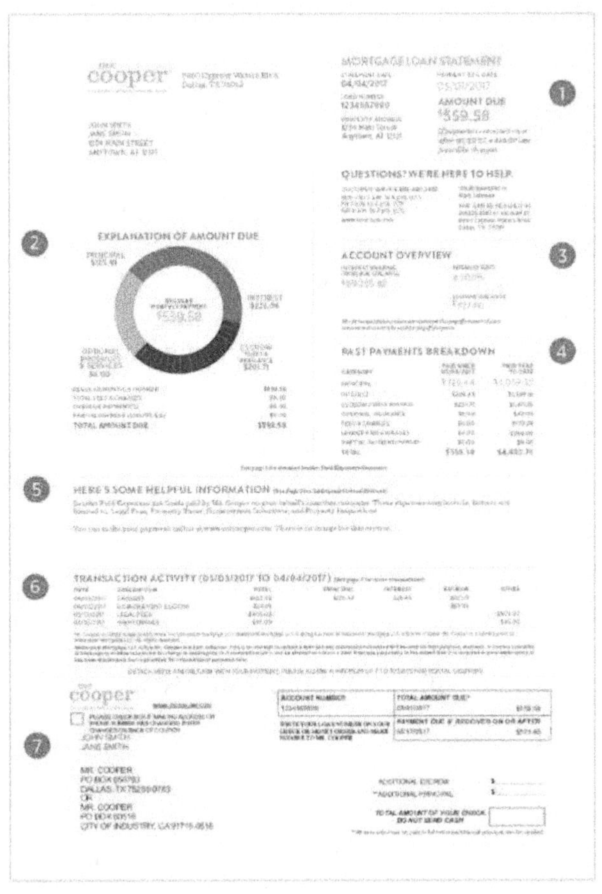

DO YOU HAVE LENDER PAID EXPENSES?

If you have any expenses that we paid to maintain and process your home loan, like legal fees, repair costs, or property inspections, then you'll see these on the second page of your statement. Click here to see an example.

If you are purchasing and financing a new home and you are in your 40s and 50s, then a 15-year term may be better, so it pays your mortgage off by retirement.

Take out a Home Equity Line of Credit (HELOC) for home improvements that maintain or improve the value of the home. I use one. Do not open a HELOC account to pay for European vacation! I only use it for home improvements. I purchased a new roof, new central heat and air system and other important and intelligent upgrades to my house. I justify this because the house is worth more than we paid for it. The investment return exceeds the cost. At the time I started the HELOC, we did not have a "pot to hiss in." (Figure it out. Think snake) We borrowed a reasonable amount of our equity for necessities. Many of my neighbors, in contrast, borrowed as much as they could during the 2008 housing bubble. The market fell off a cliff, leaving many homeowners owing more than their houses were worth. Their HELOC payments used variable interest rates and, like an Otis Elevator, their payments skyrocketed. As the economy melted, neighbors lost their jobs. They gave up paying their mortgages and HELOCS to live mortgage free until the repo man caught up with them. Welcome to the 2007-2009 financial crises. My wife and I did not lose our jobs. Your combined mortgage balance and HELOC should never exceed your home's worth.

Selling Your House

It requires special skills to sell your house.

Again, hire a reputable, experienced sales agent. Negotiate your sales commission. Yes, the sales commission is negotiable! Spend a little money to make your house look like a home someone would want to buy and live in. No need to hire a professional. Stage the house yourself. Clean out the clutter. Put stuff in storage. Clean the place. Paint the interior. Don't skimp here. If you know potential buyers are visiting, bake cookies! It's always a deal winner. Calculate, before listing your home, the total cost of marketing your house. Make sure the house price is correct. Use a source like Zillow, https://www.zillow.com/, to find out what homes in your neighborhood are selling for, before you sit down with the listing agent. Visit your county property appraiser office. They have a record of the sales in your area and by law the information is in the public record. That's how Zillow gets the info.

Personal Journal

My preteen experience with Florida Real Estate. Contract for Deeds.

When I was twelve, my family lived in rural north Florida. Retirees populated the community. I made friends with one of our elderly neighbors and was excited to find out that one of his grandchildren was about my age. We had a great time running around the neighborhood doing what kids do. On one of his visits, he mentioned to me in a bratty tone that his parents owned my property. I said politely, "You are mistaken." "AM not." Funny thing is that I maturely went to his grandfather and asked him what his grandson meant. He said that his son, my friend's father, had purchased a tax certificate on our lot. I said thank you and at once went home to tell my father.

What happened was, we lived on the lot that was purchased via contract for deed. The price was $25.00 down and $25.00 per month. In the 70s, in Florida at least, this was a very popular way to sell unwanted vacant land. We, however, had improved the property by adding a septic tank and power pole and added our beautiful doublewide mobile home. My parents were very thankful for my report and went to the real estate developer to discuss real estate taxes. When you buy a property contract for deed, the actual warranty deed does not transfer until satisfaction of the contract. Until then, the original developer/owner is still responsible for paying the real estate taxes. The developer/owner may own hundreds of vacant lots owing to small amounts of real estate tax on each lot. The game is to wait until the last minute to pay the tax or wait until the developer gets caught not paying them on contracted lots like ours. The developer understood our plight and paid the real estate taxes. Tax certificate void. I do not know why my neighbor's son did this to our lot, as there were dozens of parcels in the same subdivision that were vacant and had unpaid taxes. I told my playmate, that no, I was not mistaken, his father did not own our lot. Our friendship waned after that brief episode. Although, that same dad took the neighborhood kids out to learn how to shoot guns. The reward for exemplary behavior was shooting an M1 rifle. Ahhhh… life in the country! Yes, it was outstanding! I was twelve!!

The moral of the story is to be careful of "Contract for Deed" purchases. The advantages are in the seller's favor. If you agree to this type of contract, know the advantages and disadvantages. If your income, credit score, or location of the home is not worthy of conventional financing, then the contract for deed could be an alternative. The property is not in your name until you pay the contract in full. Be careful. It's like "buy here, pay here" car buying situation. Miss a payment and the actual owner will repossess "your" property. They are not obligated, in most states, to return your paid investment. The actual owner handles the real estate taxes. If the deed holder does not pay the real estate taxes, you risk losing your land if they sell a tax deed against your property. The property changes possession and you lose your investment.

https://www.trustedchoice.com/insurance-articles/home-family/buying-house-on-contract/

https://www.rocketlawyer.com/article/what-is-a-contract-for-deed-ps.rl

Mobile Home Parks

If you live in a mobile home in a mobile home park, then buyer beware. I just sold a double-wide mobile home for my elderly father, and what a carnival! The buyers must be pre-approved by the park management before the sale is legit. Even after the property sold, I am still paying a pro rata share of the real estate taxes. The mobile home park owners pass through to the tenants their pro rata share of the real estate taxes of their lot. A lot they rent. A lot for which they pay lot rent. Yes, on top of the lot rent, they pay a lump sum real estate tax for their share of the property they rent at the end of the year—for property they don't own. It's perfectly legal!

If you are shrewd, figure out how to become a mobile home park owner! If it's a retirement mobile home park, it's a cash cow, on the back of pensioners!

Who's My Landlord?

Does the house you are renting really belong to the landlord? During the 2008 financial crises, there were many cases where landlords learned they were upside down financially in their investment property. Their mortgage balance was more than the value of the property. The bad economy also pushed rents down, resulting in the rental income being less than the debt service (and total expenses to maintain the home investment) so savvy owners just stopped paying the mortgage payment knowing that the financial crises resulted in banks taking two years or longer to foreclose on the property mortgage. During the two or more-year period, the "owner/landlord" of the house kept collecting the rent and stuffing it in their pocket. Then, when the bank was ready to foreclose, they would inspect the house and let the tenant know they were no longer welcome in the house. The house was in foreclosure and being sold on the market. This happened with no notice and no empathy for the tenant. They were innocent victims. The law (The Protecting Tenants at Foreclosure Act of 2009) states that the tenant may complete the lease or rental agreement. However, your new landlord is the bank. Tenant beware in a poor real estate market!

The Answer to Affordable Housing, The Mobile Home…On Your Land

The mobile home or manufactured home came about because of the original travel trailer. In the 50s and 60s, as travel trailers got bigger, people lived in them as a substitute for an apartments and small homes.

In 1976, manufactured homes met FHA standards. They manufactured the above mobile home in 1972. I took the photo. It is the mobile home I grew up in. Experts consider mobile homes personal property that depreciate like a motor vehicle. Construction standards have improved, and now the construction standards resemble the quality of traditionally built homes. Mobile homes usually depreciate while traditionally built homes appreciate. However, better built, late model mobile homes can maintain their value or increase in value during a shortage in available home inventory. Mobile homes are set up on owner's land or placed in a mobile home park. Mobile homes provide an affordable alternative to traditional homes. Buy a mobile home if you are looking to reduce your housing expenses so you can pay off more debt and then save more. As soon as your finances are secure, buy a traditional house. They rise in value by the rate of inflation. In a "hot market" they can appreciate at a higher rate. Traditional houses are foundations to building family wealth.

Move Often and Lose a Fortune:

Major sources on the Internet say that the average cost of a local move is $1,250. I base this estimate upon a 2-3-bedroom household or about 7,500 pounds of stuff. Moving from state to state is closer to $5,000. A ballpark method of measuring your potential moving expense, including sales commission and moving expense, is 10% of the value of the house. This equals about 6% commission and a 4% moving fee.

It will be difficult for you to accumulate savings, let alone wealth, if you move every six months regardless of reason.

Here are some money-saving tips for moving:

1. Get estimates and shop movers who have references and great reviews. Check your moving company. There are lots of resources online to help create a moving budget. Reserve about six weeks before moving date.

2. Check out AAA Moving Discounts.

3. Find donated boxes. Don't spend too much on packing supplies. It is expensive but convenient to buy your moving supplies from a rental truck moving center.

4. Create a packing plan. Figure out what you will keep, throw away, give to friends or give to charity. Take only what you need. Moving useless, valueless stuff is not smart. Give stuff away by listing it for free on Craigslist or giving it to charity.

5. Measure all the doorways. Don't pack a box that's bigger than the doorway of your existing place or your new one.

6. Mark the contents clearly on the outside of your boxes.

7. Don't pack boxes too heavy.

8. Treat your movers nicely. This pays dividends later.

9. Don't forget to change your address.

10. Cancel old services and begin new services.

http://www.merriman.com/family-talk/moving-considerations/

<u>Personal Journal and Conclusion</u>

While still in college, I took a real estate course because of an article I read in Reader's Digest. The article explained how real estate creates the wealthiest people in the world. It sold me. I grew up in a rural and poor community. While taking the course, I lost my busboy job. I approached my real estate instructor, and he offered me a job. He hired me to clean rental properties and to do research for real estate appraisals. In six months, I earned my real estate salesperson license and did property management to earn a base salary. In addition, in my spare time, I performed real estate appraisals and began selling property. Making a living in real estate is not for the fainthearted. The good news is that there is no ceiling to your income. There is also no floor to your income. I learned most of the lessons mentioned in this chapter from the amazing time I spent in real estate while going to college. If I had not read that Reader's Digest article, I would have missed a lot of exceptional experiences.

The Real Estate Office Staff, including the author, "On Safari" on a 12,500-acre ranch.

I hear personal finance gurus and other celebrities boasting about their real estate finance success. Remember, their success resulted from very hard work. Real Estate investing and being a real estate agent is not an easy-to-get rich path. Both activities require the ability to negotiate fluidly, think on your feet, and possess an extensive amount of knowledge.

Chapter 6

Real Estate

Summary Questions

Exercise Time: approximately 25 minutes.

I. *List the pros and cons of renting a home versus buying a home.*

II. *On a piece of paper or on a spreadsheet application, list all the expenses associated with home ownership. Will this exercise help you take the prospect of working and "earning a living" more seriously?*

III. *What are the pros and cons of having roommates help share the expenses of owning or renting a house? Once you have answered it, I want you to consider a few things we learned.*

A. What is subleasing?

B. Will your landlord allow you to sublease?

C. What does the "roommate" agreement look like?

IV.   *Why is it important to understand the location of a property prior to buying it? What are examples of risky locations of house.*

V.   *What are the costs associated with breaking your lease.*

VI.   *Are mortgage brokers always acting in your best interest? What prevents them from lending you more than you can afford to pay back?*

VII.   *Create a list of all the professionals connected with a successful real estate transaction.*

VIII.   *Would you want a career in real estate or not? If yes, what's the first step you think one should take to mark a good start in real estate.*

A brief assignment!

1. *Go online to https://www.zillow.com/ and research your hometown home values.*

2. *Go online to https://www.realtor.com/ and plug in your school, city, zip into the search bar.*

3. *Go to your county Property Appraiser's office website. Google it! Visit it! It is a public office. Remember to be respectful. The Property Appraiser is a State Constitutional Officer. Yes, just like the sheriff.*

4. *Discuss with your class or group any situation you have experienced regarding housing acquisition. It is possible to learn many things from others and your experiences.*

Chapter 7

Automobiles

"You Aren't What You Drive, High net worth individuals believe that financial independence is more important than displaying high social status."

— Dr. Thomas Stanley, author, The Millionaire Next Door

Post-COVID note

In late 2022, the automobile market is a seller's market because of an influx of government stimulus increasing demand and a chip shortage hindering automobile manufacturing, which reduces supply. I predict by the end of 2022 the market will get back to normal.

The American love affair for the automobile is still insatiable. *American Graffiti* is a cult classic film that embodies this love affair. My father composed a list of the cars he owned in his life. The number is 40! As we will discuss, cars do not make wonderful investments.

My dad created this record of the cars he owned and the miles he drove them. Cycling through cars can be an expensive habit.

YR	MAKE	COST	MILEAGE
1. 1953	Pontiac (1947)	500	5000
2. 1954	Hudson	2100	42000
3. 1957	VW	1700	19000
4. 1958	Vauxhall	2000	14000
5. 1959	M-B 190d	3400	40000
6. 1961	M-B 220S	4800	29000
7. 1962	Peugeot 404	2400	55000
8. 1965	Datsun	2000	13000
9. 1966	Toyota Crown	2200	55000
10. 1967	Fiat 124	1900	29000
11. 1969	Toyota Crown	3100	29000
12. 1970	Mazda 1800	2100	104,000
13. 1971	Renault R-16	2900	55,000
14. 1973	Mazda RX-2	3900	67,000
15. 1976	Toyota Corona	4600	56,000
16. 1978	Datsun 510	5000	15,000
17. 1978	Mazda RX-4	6800	70,000
18. 1980	Volvo DL	9700	265,000
19. 1978	Mazda GLC	9800	30,000
20. 1980	Mazda GLC	6800	48,000
21. 1985	Isuzu I-mark X	8800	20,000
22. 1986	Isuzu PUP	9600	58,000
23. 1987	Ford Aerostar	15000	60,000

YR	MAKE	COST	MILEAGE
24. 1987	Volvo	15000	43,000
25. 1989	Jeep P-up	15000	40,000
26. 1991	Ford P-up	14000	66,000
27. 1991	Mazda MPV	15000	40,000
28. 1993	Chevy Van	18000	40,000
29. 1995	Chevy P-up	12500	86,000
30. 1995	Plymouth Van	16000	60,000
31. 1996	Geo Prism	16000	98,000
32. 1999	Ford Taurus	18000	35000
33. 2001	Mazda Tribute	24000	4000
34. 2001	Mazda 626	17900	29500
35. 2002	Mazda Trib	23000	50000
36. 2005	Suzuki Forenza	17000	
37. 2006	Mazda 5	17000	17000
38. 2007	Suzuki XL7	22000	60000
39. 2010	GMC	27000	27000
40. 2014	Fiat	25000	10000

The solution is to buy a 2-year-old car and replace it after you have owned it for four to eight years. Financial experts say you could save enough money, with less "auto buy cycling," to retire five years earlier. Ten-year-old cars start to "wear out (literally) their welcome" with increasing repairs. In addition, you are also getting behind in safety technology. The average age of cars in the U.S. is 11.5 years. Ten years is a good time to update. Financially, this is golden. Check out these sites to discover the total cost of car ownership:

https://www.nerdwallet.com/blog/loans/total-cost-owning-car/

https://autocosts.info/US.

Owning an automobile can be a complicated business for the inexperienced. Car ownership is not for sissies. Get someone with experience to help you navigate the choppy waters of finance related to automobile ownership. So, I know you can figure this out.

Go Online: Buy your car from a reputable online car dealership. Check out Carvana, CarMax, and the new kid on the block, Driveway. Driveway is different because they offer services besides buying, trading, and selling cars. You still have to do your homework. You still have to know your credit score in advance, research the insurance cost of your new ride, and through KBB or Edmunds, determine the value of your trade and the car you are buying. Continue reading for a little fatherly advice.

Automobile expense is the second largest expense for most people. In 2017, according to NerdWallet, average car ownership costs were over $8,000 per year if you drove 15,000 miles. Purchasing a car involves added expenses: insurance, maintenance, repairs, and gas. Many people love the "new car" smell. That smell is expensive. Most cars lose 25% of their value in depreciation the first year. I witnessed a situation where the owner of a car totaled their new

Chevrolet Camaro. They ended up owing the bank $2,000 because the car insurance paid them the car's value, not the amount of the car note. They lost their car and ended up with a $2,000 personal note owed to the bank for the difference. The car had to be replaced. Their situation was desperate. Car insurance pays the depreciated value of the car, not what you paid for your car. You get to pay the difference between the insurance company payment and your loan balance. Protect your investment with gap insurance. Buy a replacement cost auto policy.

The automobile industry is brainwashing you into purchasing a new car. The automobile industry spent $36 billion dollars worldwide on automobile advertising in 2019. According to Zenith, an ad agency think tank, the US market is worth $18 billion per year. Here's how that affects you–if you take the advertising dollars spent by a vehicle manufacturer, the number ranges from a whopper of $8,500 for each Alfa Romeo sold in the U.S. compared to $250 per Honda or Toyota. GM and Ford together spent over $5.5 billion per year to get you to turn your head.

You are being manipulated, by design!

The Dealership Experience

Personally, avoid the dealership. The only constructive purpose of the car dealership is to test drive an actual car. Don't buy the car at the dealership. Hire a car buying service from your local credit union or wholesale club. Check with AAA. They have a car buying service, too. Tell them what you want and let them work with the dealership. Buy a car from a private seller. That's how the wealthiest Americans buy a car. If you are buying a used car, CarMax is trustworthy with no finance manager to pick your pocket. If you must walk into the dealership to negotiate a price, do your homework in advance!

See below related paragraph: **I have to Buy a Car from a Dealer**

Know your credit score! Pre-arrange your auto financing. I once got a great deal because I walked in with the check written from my credit union. I negotiated as if I had cash in my pocket. Sorry, Ms. Sales Associate, I only have $16,800 in my pocket. Not a penny more.

At the beginning of the negotiations, get a number proposal from the sales associate. When the salesperson returns, ask them, "Is that the best you can do?" When the salesperson returns, look at the number, shake your head and say, "I'll have to think it over." Go through the awkward, "meet the manager" routine and LEAVE the property. Come back a month later, preferably at the end of the month, and test the same model you like again. Repeat this as many times as you can to wear the dealer down, and not the other way round! Shop at the end of the model year to secure better deals and higher rebates.

Buying a car is hard work!!!

The Finance Office at The Dealership

Here is a link to a great car loan calculator:

https://communityfirstfl.balancepro.org/resources/calculators/car-loan-calculator

The dealership finance guy is not your friend!

You are not, under no circumstances obligated to buy any product or service offered to you by the finance person. They are there to upsell you and give added profit to the dealership.

Keep silent in this office. Do not nod or move your hands. In fact, sit on your hands. Do not buy the permanent Rain X, Fabric Protector Package, Muffler Bearing Warranty (I made that up),

Manufacturer Extended Warranty, Paint Sealant, Rustproofing, Credit Life Insurance, GAP Insurance (most popular product pitched), Auto Insurance, Theft Protection VIN Etching, and/or document and delivery fees. Do not let the finance manager renegotiate your deal. Don't let them change the interest rate, down payment, monthly payment, or term of loan unless they change in your favor (very rare). If they try, walk away! I have watched finance managers physically shake when I whipped out my… wait for it… my financial calculator, and checked the figures. Several times they were wrong. On those occasions, their entire finance contract was retyped or reprinted before we moved forward.

Beware of the Yo-Yo or Spot Delivery Scam. I unknowingly bought a new car off the lot that was sold to an earlier buyer on the Yo-Yo plan. Later in the day I realized, on closer inspection, that there was a homemade CD in the CD player. I turned around to see faint red Kool-Aid stains on the back seat and the floor. The last straw was the ashtray. It was full of ashes. I brought the car back at once. It was used and abused.

The Yo-Yo goes like this: you have shaky credit, but the dealer/finance manager has access to subprime car loan money from a financial institution. The dealer tells the customer to take the car home (puppy dog sales technique) before they have signed the final documents. This is before the customer has received financial approval. "The loan is pending." This takes the customer out of the car buying market. It gets the customer excited about their new car. Then the dealer calls back, sometimes a week later, to ask you to come back to sign the paperwork, but there is a catch. You are not approved, or your payment has soared. It's suboptimal! It's immoral, but it still exists in the marketplace. Again, arrange your own financing in advance. Consider financing from a credit union. They offer lower rates and superior customer service. That takes a big hassle out of the car buying circus.

You Just Have to Buy a Car from a Dealer

Take your time purchasing your next car. Do the research. Investigate alternative dealers, cars, and lenders **before** stepping onto a car lot. It's all online. First, find the value of your next car through Kelley Blue Book www.kbb.com, and Edmunds www.Edmunds.com. NADA is another resource, http://www.nadaguides.com/Cars. Check out Carvana.com and Vroom.com to get a feel for how much you will spend on the car of your choice. If you are brave, use one of these trendy services. The downside is that there is no opportunity for negotiation. The price is the price. You do not see the car in advance. You should reserve this method for mature audiences.

Investigate the auto insurance rate on your car model. The insurance on a Cadillac Escalade may be more expensive than the Toyota Corolla. In fact, car insurance rates jump when the vehicle value exceeds $30,000. The top three least expensive cars to insure, according to a Value Penguin auto insurance report, are the Honda CRV, Chrysler Pacifica and the Honda Odyssey. Shop between insurance companies. Keep your driving record impeccable. It affects what you pay on insurance. Even minor traffic tickets will affect your auto insurance expense. If you are under 25, then you have no business owning/driving a new car. It's possible the insurance premium will be more expensive than your car payment. Save money on car insurance by adjusting your collision and comprehensive deductible. Compare insurance quotes from several insurers. Start your journey at Gabi.com https://www.gabi.com/ or TheZebra.com https://www.thezebra.com/.

Improving your credit score can reduce your insurance premiums. According to Value Penguin, the difference between a good and poor credit score can affect premiums 70%.

https://www.valuepenguin.com/state-of-auto-insurance-2021

https://www.valuepenguin.com/best-and-cheapest-cars-insure

Second, negotiate the financing in advance before walking onto a car lot, with a lender separate from the dealer. Go to your credit union in advance and get pre-approved. Do not rely on your lender to approve you for a realistic loan amount based on your budget. They will pre-approve you for an unrealistic high loan amount unrelated to your needs. Lenders are in the business to make money, not to help you with your budget! Make sure you plan your auto expense budget in advance. In 2010, they approved me for $40,000. I spent $16,800.

Get a great interest rate when you finance a car. Banks rate your interest rate upon your credit rating. Know your FICO score. Order a free copy of your credit report before you go shopping. https://www.annualcreditreport.com/index.action

The auto lenders use an "Auto-Enhanced" score which looks at auto loan specific risk. It is okay if this looks different from your regular scores.

Get copies of the three credit reports at no charge. Don't fall for the first website that comes up in the Google search. It says free credit report, but this is not the website you want. Insist upon https://www.annualcreditreport.com.

See Chapter Five: Credit Reports (if you have got a copy of Get WalletWise book with you), if no, then visit my site at www.walletwise.org for additional resources.

Third, learn how to negotiate and buy a car at a price below its (depreciated) blue book value. (Should you go to negotiating school first? Check-out https://www.scotworkusa.com/to take a negotiating class. Find a financial coach in your area who will aid you in the car buying process). Remember the seven best words in the world: "Is that the best you can do?" Put the dealer on the defensive. Sales associates take negotiating and sales classes to improve their bottom line at the cost of your bottom line. Money does not care who it belongs to. A good sales associate sees that "their" money is in your pocket. They will use every "professional" trick in the book to lighten your purse as much as possible. Take notes during the negotiation phase. You will refer to them later and this puts the salesperson on notice; don't fool around with this customer–they write everything. Negotiate each part of the deal separately. What do I mean? Do you have a trade? Negotiate the trade separately from the car purchase. Research the value of your trade online. I negotiate the purchase of the newer car first as if I have no trade. If I have a trade, I sell it to a private buyer. It is a hassle, but you will receive the retail price for your trade. Although this would depend on if the car is in good shape. If your trade needs a little mechanical or body shop makeover, then a trade could be beneficial to you and the dealer. The dealer can repair your well-worn trade at wholesale in the company garage. Bring the trade in after you have a signed contract for the newer car. A reputable dealer will honor the new car contract and give you a good deal for your trade. You risk another round of intense negotiations using this method and, ultimately, no deal. This method is for the seasoned car buyer. An alternative is taking your trade to CarMax and selling it outright for cash. I have done this and experienced a smooth, fair transaction.

The dealership will want to combine everything into a nice, neat package for "your convenience." New car, trade-in, and financing wrapped up in a neat little package. The package method is not for your convenience; the package method is for their largest profit. Fourth, learn to be unemotional during the negotiation phase. The dealer will try to convince you that the car you are buying is the last car on the planet. It is not. The dealer will explain that your research is flawed. I have heard statements such as, "Well, Kelley Blue Book is not here to buy your car" which means KBB's numbers do not show the local market. True, the dealership is not bound by any external auto appraisal service. Don't trust the dealer statement, "Here is the invoice, and you are killing me with such a lowball offer! If I honor this deal, I will have to go out of business." That statement and the invoice the dealer shows you are a joke. Dealers receive monetary incentives behind the scenes that never make it to the invoice. The invoice is a good place to negotiate.

If this dealer is not in the mood to make a deal, fine. Find a different car at a different dealership. Walk. It is the best negotiation weapon. No Deal!

Know what you can afford and don't budge. Everyone in the car buying process will encourage you to "live a little". This means you can afford to spend "a little" more. It won't hurt. Don't cave. Stick to your budget.

At the time of writing, over 7 million auto borrowers are delinquent (over 90 days late). The banker received their commission, the car sales associate received their commission, and the dealer received their profit. There is little consequence to these assistants because of your delinquent loan. Money flows out of your wallet and into their wallet. Time for you to pay the piper.

The Best Warranty

The best warranty out here is to buy reliable, reputable, brand name cars. If you buy used, have the car inspected by your mechanic. I have never bought an extended warranty.

More Automobile Finance

When financing an automobile, I recommend using a credit union. They have the most competitive interest rates, lowest GAP (guaranteed auto protection) insurance rates and best customer service. Go in, open an account, and then get pre-approved for your automobile buy. The credit union will give you a check in advance with the pay to the order field blank! They make the check amount to a predetermined amount. Negotiate the best deal you can, as if you are paying cash. Some credit unions offer buyer services that can negotiate an excellent deal for you for a reasonable fee. There are lots of goodies to enjoy when dealing with your local credit union. If the car you buy offers an added rebate using the auto manufacturer's retail credit arm, then use the manufacturer's finance company, and then refinance through the credit union. Sneaky, I know. I have done this several times. In addition, your credit union may have a car buying concierge or buying service. Most services are free; the dealership pays the car broker; your representative negotiates a great deal for you without you having to put up with the hassle of a dealership. My credit union has an easy online application!

Check out www.AAA.com, www.AutoFinder.com, or www.usaa.com if you are/were in the military.

Cash is King

The best way to own a car is to purchase it with cash. The best place to buy a car is from an individual. Obviously, do your homework and know the specific car you want to buy and know its value. Cars selling below $10,000 may be high mileage and more hassle than they are worth. Check out http://www.jdpower.com/ or www.edmunds.com to decide vehicle reliability.

You should checkout your local Facebook Marketplace to find great car deals. I found drivable used cars that had life left in them. Be careful, though, dealers will also advertise on Facebook Marketplace. That may still be ok. They know you want a "buy from an individual" experience and may play nice.

If you plan to buy an automobile with higher mileage, your best bet is Honda. I drove a 1997 Honda CRV with 178,000 miles. It's still in the family. Be prepared for repair bills, though. If you chose this route, find a great local mechanic. They are priceless. Try Yelp online. Ask friends, neighbors, and relatives for a reference. Try www.ASE.com. Finding a talented mechanic is worth the time and research. If buying an older car, consider AAA membership.

Check www.carvana.com. I also like Kia and Hyundai products, as they are inexpensive, very reliable, and come with an amazing warranty that is transferrable to the second owner. According to Hyundai/Kia, the second owner inherits the 5-year 60,000-mile part of the warranty. Find a model with 40,000 miles or fewer and you will have a good part of the warranty remaining to make sure you don't end up with large repair expenses. Find a brand you know and stick with it. I have friends who favor Toyota RAV 4s. This is smart. You know how they drive and when it is time to replace your car; you know what to expect. Stay away from cars whose earlier life was a rental car. I have found cars on Carvana with less than 10,000 miles and in excellent new condition. The sweet spot for depreciation is 3 years. You can find a multitude of "cars" (not trucks) coming off of lease contracts that are 3 years old and 36,000 miles on the odometer. Popular terms for car leases are 3 years, 12,000 miles per year. The depreciation has peeled off 50% of that new car price and if you choose wisely, you still may smell a bit of "new car" smell. So, the message here is don't lease… purchase. Buy a car that is three years old and enjoy the three-year depreciation sweet spot. Let someone else pay for the enormous loss of value to the car. (The lessee paid the depreciation in their payment). If you are a savvy negotiator and deal maker, look for local deals on eBay. A recent search on eBay produced excellent results, and the cars were in my neighborhood. Check your local credit union for community car sales. The credit union allows approved car dealers to show off their best cars on the lender's property. Since the sale is on the lender's property, the dealers have to play nice.

HMMM. I wonder if banks that lease cars make profits deducting (for their tax purposes) 50% appreciation from their corporate income tax burden. Yes, this is true.

In fact, most of your lease payment pays for your leased vehicle's depreciation. There is also interest paid, and it's called the "Money Factor" or "Lease Fee." It's how they come up with the payment!

https://www.carpaymentcalculator.net/calcs/auto-lease.php Shows Depreciation.

https://www.edmunds.com/calculators/car-lease.html Shows Detail.

Remember, leasing a car is renting long term. You have fewer rights to the car. Restricted mileage, rigid requirements for auto insurance, sales tax paid every month, and what if you want out early? Open your wallet time!

myFico has a calculator you can use to compare the costs of purchase and lease. Using the default information, the buy choice ended up costing $1400 less per year. Plug in your numbers to find out how much more auto-leasing may cost you.

https://www.myfico.com/credit-education/financial-calculators/vehicle-leasing-vs-buying

Check out the Simpson's episode when Homer leased the famed Canyonero?

Car Salesman: Here's how your lease breaks down. This is your down payment, then here's your monthly, and here is your weekly.

Homer: And that's it, right?

Car Salesman: Yup… then after your final monthly payment there's the routine CBP, or Crippling Balloon Payment.

Homer: But that's not for a while, right?

Car Salesman: Right?

Homer: Sweet!

Look at Dr. Thomas Stanley's nuggets of wisdom donned from his research conducted when authoring his book, *The Millionaire Next Door.* 20% of millionaires are "used" vehicle shoppers. They enjoy purchasing cars via "aggressive shopping among private owners, dealers and leasing companies, etc."

When Dr. Stanley wrote this, most people looked at the want ads of newspapers. The Internet was in its infancy. Sites like www.car.com, www.carvana.com, www.truecar.com, now makes finding a reliable car easier than ever before.

Be wary of Certified Used Cars. The hype sounds great. Your favorite dealer has done a 1400-point inspection on your cream puff and "stands" behind your new purchase. Certified pre-owned means they add a $1,000-$1,200 onto the price of the car for an extended warranty. When shopping for a used car with my daughter, I test drove a car with shaky brakes. They needed to be addressed. It was a "Certified" model. I returned the car to the dealer and said I "may" be interested, but the brakes needed repair. The sales agent texted later, telling me their mechanics thought the car's brakes were fine. I am sure he'll find a less informed buyer (sucker) to buy the car. Don't be a sucker. ALWAYS get the car checked out by a mechanic before you buy!

Are you interested in an extended warranty? Buy it from your credit union. They sell reasonably priced extended warranties.

My credit union website has links to NADA and Annualcreditreport.com. This credit union has budgeting information on the full cost of your car and GAP insurance.

Insurance

What is GAP insurance? If you must buy and finance a new car at 100% of the purchase price and the most popular model to impress people who don't even like you, then you may as well prepare to owe more money than the car is worth. I knew a tenant that flipped (in an accident) a new Trans Am. The completed paperwork showed that they had a $3,000 personal note owed to the bank to pay the difference between the balance owed on the car note versus the insurance payout. AND they had to buy a new car.

Gap Insurance (Guaranteed Asset Protection)

Automobile Gap Insurance is a product designed to ensure the difference between what you owe on your auto loan balance and what the car is worth. It's for car purchases that leave you "upside down" on the deal. You owe more than your car is worth. Your auto insurance company pays, in a total loss scenario, the book value of the car only. When you buy a car new off the lot, its value can drop 50%. Often the value is below what you owe on the car. Have a total loss and the insurance company will pay you what they think the car is worth. This is an opportunity to negotiate. You don't have to accept what the insurance company is offering. Remember these seven words! "Is that the best you can do?" Often, insurance companies will increase their payout. Remember, they are buying the car from you. Remember, they will take your "totaled" car, repair it and sell it, or sell it to a junkyard for scrap. To insure against this situation, you can buy an added "GAP" insurance policy. Never buy from the car dealership. Like any purchase you make, SHOP! In my experience, the best deal on GAP insurance is through your credit union. If you must buy a new car, be an excellent negotiator. If you need GAP insurance, then you may need to take another auto purchasing and negotiating course.

> Too many people spend money they earned… to buy things they don't want… to impress people that they don't like. — Will Rogers

Buy Here, Pay Here.

OK. Your FICO credit score is below 600 and no reputable credit union or bank will finance you. You have no cash? You have no job or live on social security. You are a subprime borrower. What do you do? You may be in the market for a "Buy Here, Pay Here lot". It means a used car dealership with 10 to 15+ year-old cars with high mileage and a high probability of needing a repair soon. I visited a local BHPH lot, and they have cars that need a lot of TLC. I found a 2000 Saturn SL2. The price was $800 down and $87.50 per week. The car's radio was missing. It had 200,000 hard miles on it. The USC Trojans license plate added to my confidence in this "Cream Puff" as this car spent some time belonging to a college student. They sell cars with no warranty. You buy "as is." The dealer allows you to take the car to a mechanic to inspect. The car may be worth $500 cash. I don't understand why these places exist. The down payment is more than the same car for sale in better condition, cash! I found a 2001 Saturn SL for $1,500 that looked great. Car was in good condition and the accessories worked. Check for clean title. That's not always a given.

Put as little as $1,000 down $100 per week and the finance arm of the "Buy Here, Pay Here" car dealership will be your new transportation partner. The dealership requires you to make your payment in person…every week. They install a GPS tracker to make repossession easier and a "kill" switch to disable your vehicle. Miss a payment and the dealer will be in the driveway along with a tow truck to repossess your new ride. They will take the car, clean it, put it on the lot and start over again. Selling the same car twice, three times or more is a great way to make a living! To avoid this mayhem, you may move closer to work, buy a used bicycle, and save enough money to pay cash for a "new" car... In my town, Jacksonville, Florida, there are several reputable "buy here, pay here" auto dealerships. Just remember, "If it sounds too good to be true," it is! Beware of loan contracts contingent on you purchasing add-ons such as extended warranties and auto insurance. Be careful of the scam called "Yo-Yo." Many times you think the deal is complete, but after you take the car home (fall in love with it), the dealership will call to tell you days or weeks later that you do not qualify for the agreed to terms and you must raise your auto loan interest rate or your down payment. Don't be a victim. Try to buy a good used car with cash!

In addition, there is legal recourse. When you buy a "Buy Here, Pay Here" car, receive legitimate paperwork. Dealerships may obey the Truth in Lending Act. However, Regulation Z states what they must include in the sales agreement. 1: That the dealership is your financial partner.

2: The dealer must show the cash price.

3. The dealer must show the total financed amount.

Be careful of online auto lenders targeting at-risk borrowers. They lend you money, and then refer you to a local Buy Here, Pay Here dealer, telling you what car you WILL buy. Beggars can't be choosers! https://www.autocreditexpress.com/

Protect yourself from a used car scam by ordering a vehicle history report from Carfax. Carfax reports the previous owners' locations, recorded accidents, and title histories. Title history shows you the salvage, flood, hail, lemon, and rebuild issues. Plug the VIN (Vehicle Identification Number, know this!) number into the NHTSA website to research any Safety Issues & Recalls.

Here is a picture of my cream puff from a few years ago after a discussion with the sales manager that I should leave the premises.

In conclusion, I find it fascinating to discover that most millionaires don't drive European luxury cars. People who want to "look like" millionaires drive expensive European luxury cars. Only 24% of millionaires own new cars. In fact, the average American spends about 70% of what the typical millionaire pays for their most expensive vehicle. Many millionaires enjoy finding cash deals from private buyers. If you plan on becoming wealthy, do not invest in expensive new cars. Most people who own expensive new cars purchased them with cash after they became wealthy, not before they became wealthy. If you borrow to buy an expensive new car, you lower your odds of becoming wealthy.

Abridged from Stanley, Thomas J., and William D. Danko. *The Millionaire Next Door: The Surprising Secrets of America's Wealthy.* 1st Taylor Trade Pub. ed. Lanham, Md.: Taylor Trade Pub., 2010.

Learn how to negotiate before walking onto a car lot. Go to a flea market and haggle with vendors. Practice making offers on inexpensive items on eBay to get the feel of compromise or Win-Win negotiation. Take an experienced friend to the dealership to help you negotiate. Remember two things. "No Deal" is always an option. Try Win-Win. If unsuccessful, walk away from the table. Before you do, ask the seven most valuable words in the English language, "Is that the best you can do?"

Automobile Repair

Automobile repair is another opportunity to overspend. Auto repair is another industry with a shifty reputation. Without appearing to be outright scam artists, they encourage service writers to upsell. I encourage you to be familiar with your car's owner's manual and with your car's maintenance schedule. In addition, get more than one estimate if you have a large repair. It's great to have a relationship with a mechanic whom you can trust, but be careful. That trust translates into making suggestions to you for unnecessary repairs. Be careful of relying on your car dealership. They make very little income from selling cars. The vast majority of their profits come from the service department.

There is no shame in knowing a little about how an automobile operates. If you are buying a used car, you will need to check for recalls. You need to be on the ball about this because dealers may "conveniently forget" to remind you of this detail, because dealerships get a reduced rate for handling manufacturing recalls. https://www.nhtsa.gov/recalls

In working with dealership repair departments, I have had problems. They told me I needed service on an item that my owner's manual said was currently unnecessary. When I showed this info to the service advisor, they were not happy. I did not allow the service; I walked out the door.

Your relationship with a dealership service writer is a conflict of interest. Some dealerships pay service writers a 100% commission.

My Kia was pulling to the left. I took the car to my mechanic to have the alignment checked. That was not the problem. The tire wear was abnormal. Initially, I got an estimate for two new tires. I said, no, we need to submit the tires for a warranty replacement. If I had not spoken up, I would have been on the hook for an added $200 plus. If you are a woman, I would strongly encourage you to "borrow" a man to aid you in negotiations. I'm sorry. That's just how the world is today. I taught this technique to my daughter. She asked an acting student "hunk" from college to join her in retrieving her car after an unexpected repair because of negligence. Her mechanic forgot to tighten the lug nuts on one of her wheels. Funny thing was that she was in the shop to get her oil changed. The shop was pressuring my teenage daughter to buy tires. It was unnecessary. You can imagine the conversation between papa bear (me) and the service manager afterward.

Major Items of Interest on Your Car

1. Regular Oil Changes;

2. Inspect and Replace Tires when Necessary;

3. Inspect and Repair Brakes when Necessary;

4. Air Filter Every One or Two Years;

5. Windshield Wiper Blades (Most Auto Parts Stores Will Install them for you, No charge);

6. Change Coolant every 2 years (Depends on Mileage, Check Owner's Manual);

7. Transmission Fluid Change after 100,000 miles.

That's the most important stuff. These are not usually expensive maintenance items. Integrate these items into your budget as a non-repeating budget item.

Extended Auto Warranties

Automobile extended warranties can waste money sometimes. The best warranty is to buy a reliable car. Buy an affordable policy from the automobile manufacturer or your credit union. Credit Unions have the best prices. Ignore warranty companies that use telemarketers and direct mail. When you need to make a purchase, you start the conversation.

https://www.thebalance.com/warranty-scams-you-must-avoid-4135721

Here is an unwanted extended warranty pitch I received in the mail. Purchase nothing based on a sales pitch like the one below. Oh look! There is a 0% interest payment option! Whoo Hoo!

Hybrid and Electric Cars

Buy a hybrid or EV (Electric Vehicle) only if you are wealthy! The rest of us should read the above to learn how to buy a reliable and affordable used car.

Hybrids and electric cars have amazing depreciation. Electric and hybrid car owners face up to 60 and 70 percent depreciation rates over 5 years. Buy used if you want a hybrid or EV! But be careful. Buy a used one with low mileage to preserve as much warranty as possible. Make sure you receive the transferable manufacturer's warranty. This may be the time for an extended warranty.

Hyundai has a lifetime warranty on its hybrid batteries. Limited transferable warranty.

Toyota Prius is 96 months or 100,000 miles. Transferable if a car is a certified used vehicle.

Chevy Bolt: 8 years 100,000 miles.

Honda Insight: Warning, Warning! 100 month (8 years 4 months) limited warranty.

From the 2019 Honda Insight Warranty Handbook:

Warranty coverage during the first 36 months (3 years) of service, a defective replacement 12-volt battery will be replaced at no cost for the battery, labor, or installation.

For the remaining 64 months (5 years and 4 months), you will receive a credit toward the purchase of the 12-volt battery. They base this credit on the then-current retail price:

• Months 37 to 45: 60%

• Months 46 to 55: 50% • Months 56 to 65: 40%

• Months 66 to 75: 30%

• Months 76 to 85: 20%

• Months 86 to 95: 10%

• Months 96 to100: 5%

Note too self: sell the car before it's 36 months old.

I test drove the Honda Insight and I would consider purchasing one. However, their warranty leaves me worried.

The Toyota Prius is the better investment among hybrids. It is the world's first mass produced hybrid starting in 1997. It appears battery replacement is a priced maintenance issue when compared to gas cars over the life of the car. However, I have no experience. The Toyota Warranty is not limited. It's 96 months, 100,000 miles, not a prorated warranty like Honda.

2022 Update

Electric cars are becoming more mainstream, but finding charging station locations is still a struggle. The future looks interesting, but I would wait before buying an electric car.

Chapter 7

Automobiles

Summary Questions

Exercise Time: minimum 20 minutes.

Automobiles are the second most expensive purchase behind real estate before a college education became so expensive. Carefully review the following questions. After completion working on your own, begin a class discussion.

I.   *How do you feel about borrowing money to purchase a car?*

II.   *Ever had a dealership experience? If yes, share your experience!*

III.   *Do you consider the car salesperson and car dealership your friends? Are they always looking out for your best interest?*

IV.   *How do you determine if the used car you are buying is mechanically sound? List at least 2 ways.*

V.   *If you have little negotiating experience, how will you develop this skill set?*

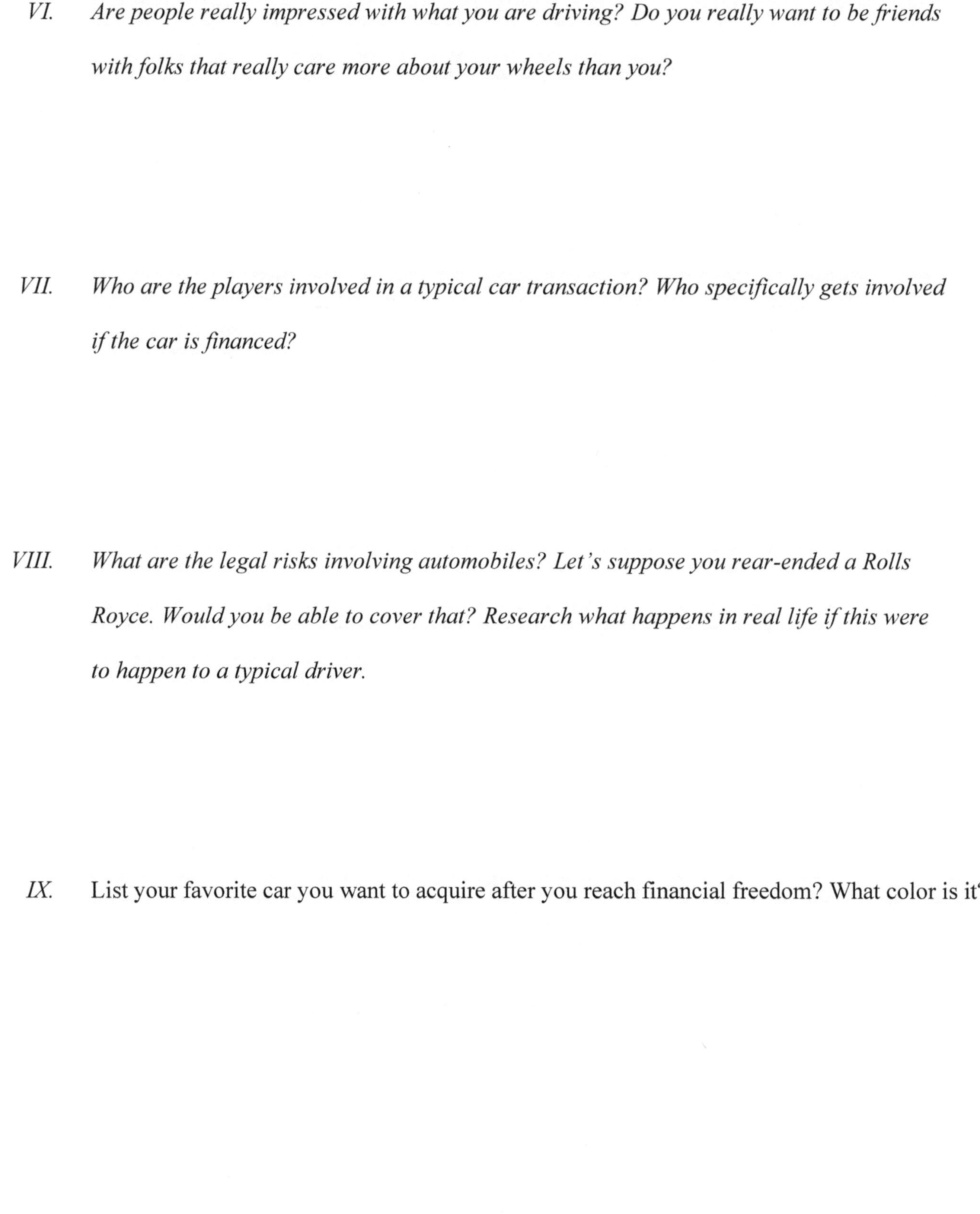

VI.   *Are people really impressed with what you are driving? Do you really want to be friends with folks that really care more about your wheels than you?*

VII.   *Who are the players involved in a typical car transaction? Who specifically gets involved if the car is financed?*

VIII. *What are the legal risks involving automobiles? Let's suppose you rear-ended a Rolls Royce. Would you be able to cover that? Research what happens in real life if this were to happen to a typical driver.*

IX.   List your favorite car you want to acquire after you reach financial freedom? What color is it?

Action Plan!

1. Visit your insurance agent to see the difference in premiums (cost of insurance) between various car models you want to buy.

2. Visit your local credit union to find out all you can about qualifying in advance for a car loan. This helps you at the negotiating table.

Chapter 8

Saving and Investing

"If you would be wealthy, think of saving as well as getting."

—Benjamin Franklin

Savings is probably the most important aspect of achieving money, balance, and wealth. I made the mistake of not saving early because I was too busy treading water financially. Instead of saving, I was buying unnecessary stuff. Don't make the same mistake.

Saving has to be painless, sustainable, and ongoing. Saving should be a regular, planned activity.

Regardless of your income, save money. Why? First, to create an emergency fund to face life's unexpected expenses down the road. Do you want to buy a house, start a business, or pay for your children's or grandchildren's college education in the future? You will want to save money to accomplish your goals. Speaking of which, what are your goals for savings? Concrete goals for savings will help you stay on track. Another significant reason to save is so we can retire without having to work.

This chapter assumes you have paid off your unsecured debt. If not, go back and read Chapter One: Credit Card Debt. Pay off unsecured debt (credit cards, personal loans, store accounts) before starting a savings strategy.

This is the WalletWise six-step plan to savings and investing!

1. Save for an emergency fund by first opening an FDIC or FCUA insured account.

Reduce Expenses to Increase Savings

Do not progress to step two until completion of step one. Go to Chapter Four, Money Management and Your Budget, to create a realistic family budget on paper. The budget will show you where to cut expenses. Open an online and mobile MINT account to track expenses in real time. Make it possible to save by implementing:

1. Negotiate Lower Prices on Necessities, like Utilities. (AskTrim);
2. Cancel Expensive Cable Subscriptions;
3. Cancel Underutilized Online Subscriptions;
4. Sell Expensive assets and replace (Can you sell your financed car and replace it with a reliable cash car?);
5. Trim Gift Expenses;
6. Take Inexpensive Vacations
7. Increase Income.

A fully funded emergency account is equal to 3-6 months of your annual salary, let's say $20,000. Safe and sound in an FDIC insured account. Save your money in a FDIC money market account and not in an uninsured money market fund!

2. Invest in your company's 401k until you qualify for your company's full match. Every 401k plan is unique. Check with Human Resources to get company match information. You will need to find the "sweet spot." The amount that triggers the maximum employer benefit. Contribute a little more. Go to Step 3 if you have deposited enough in your 401k to get your max benefit. If you do not have access to a 401k or 403b, go to Step 3.

3. Open a ROTH IRA and invest until you max out at $6,000; $7,000 if you are age 50 or older.

4. Open a Computershare Account to accumulate quality dividend-paying stocks.

5. Save for College in your state approved 529 Plan.

6. Learn how to Earn.

Estimated Time Frame: This is not a place for immediate gratification!

"The single greatest edge an investor can have is a long-term orientation. Behold the turtle. He makes progress only when he sticks his neck out. Someone's sitting in the shade today because someone planted a tree a long time ago." *–James Bryant Conant*

WalletWise Savings Timeline

Saving = 0-5 Years   Emergency Fund, Money Market Accounts

Cash Investing = 10-60 years   401k, IRAs, Mutual Funds, Index Funds, ETFs

"You can never start saving too early, but it's never too late to start." *–Ken Remsen*

Time Value of Money

It is true the earlier you save, the better. Why? Because the longer you save, the more time the money earns interest. Then it earns interest on the interest. According to Clark Howard, if a fifteen-year-old saves $2,000 per year each year for seven years (leaving it untouched), then it will accumulate to $1,020,430 by age sixty-five! Clark did not mention that these returns depend upon earning 10% interest per year. That's very possible. The point is to save early!

Here are two cool calculators I found online. Just move the sliders and it calculates the cost of delaying saving.

https://www.fireflycu.org/Calculators/Savings-Calculators/Delaying-Savings-Calculator

https://www.icmarc.org/prebuilt/static/costofdelay/index.html

Personal Note: Hey! Did you save at fifteen? Most people don't. I did not. I was too busy paying bills, figuring out how to survive, starting a business, working for a family-owned business with no benefits, and did not get serious until I was forty-three. I was not a wonderful role model. The good news is if you stay married to your first spouse or become the victim of a nasty addiction, your survival/lifestyle expenses go down as you get older, and your children leave the nest. Then you have more discretionary money to save and invest.

Now let's unpack The WalletWise Savings Plan.

Step One: Emergency Fund

Begin SAVING with an Emergency Fund.

Okay, after you have created your budget, calculated your net worth, adjusted your expenses so you spend less than you make, paid off expensive credit card debt, then you can plan to save money. The first item to create is your emergency fund. This is equal to six months' salary.

If, by any chance, you got this out of order and you have signed up for an online investment plan or club, or you are investing in your company's 401k or agency's 403b before paying off all of your credit card debt and high interest debt…STOP IT! I have worked with people who were investing with https://www.acorns.com/ or www.stash.com when they had excessive credit card debt and were insolvent. Pay off credit card and any other unsecured debt first before starting Step 1.

You cannot ignore paying off high interest credit accounts. I'm not talking about mortgage payments or even car payments. I am particularly referring to credit card debt and personal loan debt. You are paying 12, 15, 18 percent and higher interest to borrow unsecured debt. It is doubtful you earn that rate of return on your investments over the long haul. Therefore, pay off the debt first to reduce the amount of money you are spending on paying interest so you can start saving to have interest coming to you.

In my less successful years (and there were many of them!) I never understood the concept of an emergency fund. I had some money saved and used that money for emergencies. I never set aside money in an emergency fund. The purpose of an emergency fund escaped me. Make sure you know your emergency fund savings. Treat the emergency fund differently from other savings. The emergency fund is very important because it allows you to take care of emergencies without relying on predatory and expensive payday loans, car title loans, pawn shops, and checking account overdrafts to take care of your unexpected expense. Most experts agree you should save six months of your household income. If you make $50,000 per year, saving $25,000 is a lot to ask. Start by saving 10% of your income through automation in a traditional bank (FDIC) or credit union (NCUSIF) savings account. The Federal Government insures these accounts. Make sure your payment is automatic. It's called **Pay Yourself First**! That would be about $350 per month after taxes. If you cannot save this much, I suggest seeing Chapter Four: Money Management and Your Budget, to begin the road of spending less than you make. Reduce your unnecessary expenses so you can channel money into savings. It is essential.

Do not invest your emergency fund in the stock market. The emergency fund is not an investment opportunity. The emergency fund should be in a low-risk savings account. Online bank accounts offer a good safe return and fast access to your funds in case of an emergency. Bank CDs, or Certificate of Deposits, are okay, but they are more difficult to access in an emergency! This may defeat the purpose of getting money quickly in an emergency.

For Online savings I recommend Ally Bank, Marcus by Goldman Sachs, and Chime to name a few. I've had personal experience saving with Discover Bank. I managed multiple CDs and a Money Market account for a client. They have excellent customer service and pay competitive rates for an online account.

Consider a Money Market account as this gives you quick access to the funds in an emergency and provides a better-than-average interest rate.

Step Two: 401k

Now it's time to start and/or restart investing in your company 401k.

Fun Fact:

Did you know that 401k is the actual tax code number relating to this retirement plan?

Find out the minimum to invest to max out your company match. I love 401's, but many of them have high fees and limited investment options. I recommend investing the minimum amount to qualify for your full company match. After you have invested enough to get the largest corporate or company match, we can move on to the next step, Step 3. Do not invest your 401k in company stock. It's too risky. If you are under thirty, choose an aggressive growth stock index fund like Vanguard Total Stock Market Index Fund (VTSMX) or Fidelity® 500 Index Fund (FXAIX). (VTSMX and FXAIX) is the mutual fund ticker, or acronym for the fund, or the name of a corporation. For example, Coca Cola is (KO) (for knockout) Facebook is (FB) Apple is (AAPL) If you wish to be rich someday, you will want to know what these tickers represent. Mutual funds represent a basket of companies to help you diversify. They represent your access to own the world's most profitable corporations. Along with other managers, the CEO of that company now works for you, no matter how small the investment is. Companies that pay dividends return those profits they make to the shareholders as dividends. Dividends create the passive income for wealthy Americans to live without selling their labor at a regular job. (nothing wrong with that!). Make sure you select to reinvest the dividends. Reinvest the dividends and capital gains automatically to increase your investment return. You should reinvest those gains back into the mutual fund to buy more shares that…wait for it…earn more dividends for you. This is the art of compounding. The act of borrowing money uses compound interest against you. However, investing money puts compound interest in your favor!

Locate an aggressive or defensive fund, based on your investing style, from the collection of funds that your 401k allows you to purchase.

It is unnecessary for you to be the sage of Wall Street.

Step Three: IRA's

After you set up your emergency fund, and max out your 401k, it is time to set up your next investment vehicle.

Open a ROTH IRA with Vanguard. In 2021, you can contribute $6,000 per year ($7,000 if you are over 50) into a Roth IRA according to the IRS. It's tempting to open a Traditional IRA to offset this year's tax liability, but be aware. The tax savings you get today may be less than the tax bill you get tomorrow. You cannot take the money from an IRA until you are 59½ years old. This is a restriction placed on this account for income tax advantages.

Look at the headlines. The pandemic gave our government permission to speed up spending to prop up the economy at the price of going into deeper debt. We should send a copy of this book to Congress! As of today, July 2022, the national debt is over 30.5 Trillion Dollars. That's $91,778 per citizen and $243,000 per taxpayer. How's that going to get paid? Try higher taxes. I prefer the Roth IRA. Tax me now. Then, when I need to take my required minimum distribution (RMD) in retirement, my withdraw is tax free. This strategy assumes that your tax rates in the future are going up.

https://www.usdebtclock.org/

https://www.rothira.com/

https://www.irs.gov/retirement-plans/traditional-and-roth-iras

I prefer Vanguard. Why Vanguard? Followers of John Bogle's savings philosophy are called Bogleheads! He founded Vanguard Funds in 1974 based upon the notion that regular folks like you and me could be and should be investing. One quote stated in the below video is Mr. Bogle wanted "regular" folks to have a "fair shake" for investing.

Please take time to watch the video. It will be good for your financial soul.

https://about.vanguard.com/who-we-are/a-remarkable-history/founder-Jack-Bogle-tribute/

https://about.vanguard.com/who-we-are/a-remarkable-history/

Another reason I prefer Vanguard is their low fees. Mutual funds charge fees for management, legal, and accounting expenses. Lower management fees leave more money in your account to make money. They take less capital from you.

"If you have trouble imagining a 20% loss in the stock market, you shouldn't be in stocks."

–John Bogle

Remember, invest for the long haul. Yes, there are other reputable mutual fund companies like Fidelity and T. Rowe Price.

Dollar Cost Averaging

Pay an equal amount monthly to smooth out market volatility. Start by contributing $100 monthly. You pay $1,200 over twelve months and your investment is now worth $1,376. The current price of the stock rose to $81.27 per share, but you only paid $70.83 per share. That's how dollar cost averaging works. It balances out the difficulties in the market. So, timing the market is unnecessary.

Go to Step Four after you have set up your Emergency Fund, funded your 401K enough to qualify for your company match, and maxed out your IRA's.

Step Four: A Basket of Five Conservative Stocks: What is the definition of "qualified" and "unqualified" funds? As much as I believe 401ks, pension funds, and IRAs are wonderful because they delay taxation on deferred compensation, they come with rules from the government. Pensions, 401ks, and IRAs come with rules and provisos (behavior control) in exchange for tax relief. That's not a bad thing. Call it stealth "discipline." These accounts will fund your retirement. There are steep penalties for making early withdrawals. Don't withdraw $35,000 out of your Individual RETIREMENT Account to buy a new Chevrolet Camaro Z28. If you do, you receive hefty tax penalties. IRAs and 401ks have an age 59 ½ withdrawal limitation. The IRS considers these accounts "qualified."

After teaching the personal finance part of a low-level math class in high school, I learned about the entity called Computershare. It is a company that manages a collection of a corporation's Direct Stock Purchase Plans (DSPP). https://www.computershare.com/us

We call this investment "unqualified," meaning unbridled, unrestricted, and to the undisciplined, unmanageable. Withdraw and spend money, **invest** in the new Camaro with no penalties. And you will return to that infamous club, the wealth underachievers. Congratulations. Now reread this book.

I discovered Computershare in 2007. I went online and realized I could buy individual stocks from an entity called a transfer agent. This is a company that places individual stocks with individual owners and manages the dividend distribution without the use and expense of a stockbroker. SWEET! They design this savings plan for the small investor. You can invest as little as $25.00 per month without a stockbroker commission. There is a fee, but the fee is small, and you pay at setup and through automatic deductions. Research the company you wish to invest in inside the Computershare website. Corporations charge high fees for their DRIP/DSPP plan. For example, Ford ticker (F) charges a $10.00 setup fee plus 3 cents per share, purchase fee is $5.00 plus 3 cents per share, and automatic deposit is $1.00 plus 3 cents per share. Computershare has a research tool directing you to companies that do not charge purchase fees. Aqua (WTR) and Abbot (ABT) are two companies in the plan I own. In addition, your money invested here is after tax. The new earnings (dividends) are taxed at the lower than income "capital gains" tax. This is unqualified money unencumbered by the rules of 401ks and IRAs. You can make withdrawals or deposits as many times as you wish. You have total freedom. I started investing when the stock market was tanking after the financial crises. I kept my investments conservative because I realized how close we came to real national financial collapse. We were close, folks. Fortunately, that did not happen, and I could put together a nice portfolio of quality stocks for pennies on the dollar. A once in a lifetime opportunity. I only keep track of a few stocks. You should only concentrate on five. I started with MSFT, NEE, ABT, VZ, and WTR. These stocks are (DRIP) stocks, or members of a Dividend Reinvestment Plan. Computershare reinvests the stock cash dividend into more shares of the company. They have worked well in the long term. Remember, this works for me. Decide what works for you. In these accounts, I have conservative dividend-paying stocks.

https://www.sec.gov/fast-answers/answersdriphtm.html

Use part of your "investment" time to research individual stocks. Less is more. Research a stock with a familiar company, a company whose product you use. Most people use products from Exxon, Walmart, Apple, Samsung, Microsoft, McDonald's, IBM, Verizon, and AT&T. Computershare handles these companies. Computershare is not the only transfer agent. There are other transfer agents. To keep life uncomplicated, stick with one and the best, which I believe is Computershare.

How to Study a Specific Stock: First, I use a site called Investopedia.com to answer any type of general investment question. Then I check out the website of my target investment company. Let's check out Abbott laboratories, https://www.abbott.com/. I check out the company's products. Abbott has unique nutrition products for consumers. Inside healthcare, Abbott provides cardiovascular medical devices, diabetes diagnostics, nutritional supplements, and a dozen major medicines. I then check the investors tab. Abbott (ABT) makes available to us the company annual report (important), SEC filings (important, but unnecessary now), and links to receive printed material in the mail that pertains to the company and alerts by email. I sign up for alerts so I get corporate news as soon as possible. You can download the annual report to your computer. The last part of the annual report is the important part. Find the income and balance statements and learn how to read these statements.

Oh wait! Shazam! Remember, you know how! You have done this for yourself, right? You have created an income (budget) and balance statement for yourself. Same idea, just bigger numbers. So, big numbers scare you? Look in Chapter Four: Money Management and Your Budget. After you have completed your personal budget (income) and balance sheet, come back here and apply what you have learned to see if your company is financially healthy. Ask important questions about the company. Is the company making money? Can the company pay its debt? Is the company the top company in its "sector?" Google the company and see what stories pop up. Have they arrested the CEO for fraud? Has your company just secured the cure for cancer? Make sure you use reliable resources. Late-night comedians do not make reliable financial sources.

That's company number one, four more to go. Now you see why I only suggest studying **five** companies. It's actual work.

https://www.nasdaq.com/investing/dozen/   Suggestions on what to research.

https://www.kiplinger.com/   Research Resource.

https://finance.yahoo.com/

"Formal education will make you a living; self-education will make you a fortune."—Jim Rohn.

Other Investment Tools.

What's an ETF?

An ETF is another investing tool similar to a mutual fund. It holds a basket of stocks like a mutual fund. Unlike a mutual fund, we can trade an ETF like a stock. It is an alternative investment tool to a mutual fund. Mutual funds only report their value once a day. Stock values rise and fall while the markets are open, based upon their market supply and demand. ETFs are funds that work the same as individual stocks. You can buy one and sell on the same day (not wise). ETFs are in between mutual funds and individual stocks. They are safer than individual stocks because they are a diversified collection of stocks that lessen your individual stock risk. Fees may be less expensive than mutual funds. They are more liquid, meaning you can trade them as individual stocks. ETFs may offer a lower tax liability. They have a lower investment minimum. The news is that you cannot make automatic investments as you can with a mutual fund. Mutual funds allow you to make fixed automatic investments. Workplace retirement plans invest in mutual funds.

ROBOTS in Charge

The next big thing is "Robo" (short for robot) investing. It means you can invest money online into vehicles that act as your financial advisor using artificial intelligence. Fees are low and expectations are high. I use Stash to see how it works.

Here are the popular ones.

https://robinhood.com/us/en/

https://www.stashinvest.com/

https://www.acorns.com/

https://www.personalcapital.com/

https://www.blooom.com/

https://www.sofi.com/invest/

https://www.ellevest.com
(for Women)

https://intelligent.schwab.com

https://stash.com

Schwab states that they have a $5,000 minimum and their robot-advisor builds and rebalances your diversified portfolio. You answer a short questionnaire to establish your investment tolerance to risk and to decide your goals. The ROBO advisor creates your portfolio! No calculating, no research (Boo!), and no hard work. Not a bad idea, but you won't learn finance. And that may be okay.

Personal Note: I recently started using a Core Portfolio that automatically rebalances and reallocates the invested funds. As of 2021, it currently is earning 18%. Anyway, we'll see how long this good run lasts.

Step Five:

College Savings 529 Plans, Coverdell

Saving for college is not a bad idea. Saving for retirement is more important. The original program was the Coverdell Education Savings Account (ESA). The Tax Cuts and Jobs Act of 2017 make Coverdell redundant. State sponsored 529 plans are now the "go-to" tax benefit/college savings plan. In fact, 529 plans allow you to save for private K-12 tuition (up to $10,000) besides college expenses. A 529 plan, named after Section 529 of the Internal Revenue Code, is a tax-advantaged plan of saving for your child's future college expenses. Individual states sponsor 529 Savings Plans. In Florida, for example, you open this "qualified" account and begin selecting investments that fit your investment style. Use your child's future enrollment date to choose a target date style fund. The investment grows tax free, similar to a traditional IRA. You should set it up with automatic deduction. You can ask your family and friends to contribute through an **eGift portal**. The 529 plan account saves for tuition, fees, books and supplies. It is for room and board when you enroll your student at least half-time in a program. They can use the funds for computers, peripherals, software, and internet costs. The Florida plan allows you to attend any qualified public or private educational institution nationwide.

https://www.myfloridaprepaid.com/

Check to see if your state has the same opportunity.

US Savings Bond or I Bond

Another great tool for saving is the online I Bond. You can buy an "I bond" for as little as $25.00 per month. This savings tool introduces children to savings. There are directions to open a "Minor Linked Account." This is a great way to give an always appreciated gift to children from members of the family. The interest earned is very low but picks up during times of inflation. The I bond is a very slow, steady, and safe savings vehicle.

Treasury Direct is the place you come to later (after you are wealthy or have accumulated more than $500,000) to buy US Treasuries. As of late 2022, because of inflation, I Bonds were earning over 9.5% interest!

https://www.treasurydirect.gov/

Step Six:

Investment Education Resources

If you are interested in learning more about the world of personal finance and investing, please consider the following resources:

An amazing resource for investment education is the Next Generation Personal Finance Program. As a math teacher, I have taught several math courses with financial component, and this is an excellent resource. Check it out at https://www.ngpf.org/. It's full of info.

My credit union, Community First Credit Union, has an amazing financial education program called moveUP

https://www.communityfirstfl.org/move-up

https://www.cashcourse.org/   (Great Financial Management Starter Course)

https://www.aaii.com/   (Investing Education Resource)

https://www.investoreducation.org/   (Awesome for Investor Education) www.investopedia.com   (Investing Education)

www.finra.org   (Financial Regulatory Authority)

www.nasdaq.com   (Exchange and Research Resource)

https://www.sipc.org/   (Investor Protection Resource)

Is there a **Step Seven?** Yes. After you accumulate about $300,000 in assets, hire a professional money manager. This is not a topic of this book. If you achieved this goal, Congrats!

> *"Compound Interest is the eighth wonder of the world. He who understands it, earns it… he who doesn't… pays it."*
>
> *–Albert Einstein*

In Conclusion, INVEST in Yourself!

Please take time to start adulting! The wealthiest people in America take time out of their busy schedule to educate themselves, as well as manage and watch their savings, investments, and finances. This means you may have to adjust your video game and TV watching schedule. If you spend six hours a day at the local bar complaining about your poor lot in life, then you may find that adjusting your schedule and changing that habit may reap financial rewards. You reap what you sow. Farmers know this. It's called the "Law of the Harvest." For a crop to be successful, you will need good seeds, fertile soil, and enough moisture. If you sow (save) generously, you will reap (receive rewards) generously. Conversely, sow sparingly, you reap sparingly.

Mutual Funds Favorites

- FMAGX   Fidelity Magellan https://fidelity.com

- VDIGX   Vanguard Dividend Growth Fund
  - Minimum Investment $3,000 www.vanguard.com

- VGHCX   Vanguard Health Care Sector Fund (Held up well in Pandemic)
  - Minimum Investment $3,000

  - VTIAX Vanguard Total International Stock Index Fund Admiral Shares
    Minimum Investment $3,000

- VEIPX   Vanguard Equity Income Fund Investors Shares
  - Minimum Investment $3,000

- PRSCX   T. Rowe Price Science and Technology Fund. (Did Well in Pandemic)
  - Minimum Investment $2,500

- SWSSX   Schwab Small-Cap Index Fund   schwab.com
  - Minimum investment: $100

Warren Buffett's Favorite 5 Vanguard Mutual Funds

https://finance.yahoo.com/news/buffett-advice-5-vanguard-funds-194833003.html

Required Legalese!

Folks! I, Ken Remsen, am **not** offering investment advice in this book.

INVESTMENT RISKS:

Investments, including real estate, are speculative and involve a large risk of loss. We encourage our readers to invest carefully. We encourage investors to get personal advice from their professional investment advisors and to make independent investigations before acting on information published here. Much of our information derives from information published by companies or submitted to governmental agencies on which we believe to be reliable but are without our independent verification. We cannot assure you that the information is correct or complete. We do not warrant or guarantee the success of any action you take in reliance on our statements or recommendations.

Past performance is not indicative of future results. Investments carry risk and investment decisions of an individual remain the responsibility of that individual. There is no guarantee that systems, indicators, or signals result in profits or that they will not result in losses. Investors should understand risks associated with any investing they do.

Hypothetical or simulated performance is not indicative of future results. Unless noted otherwise, return examples provided in our websites and publications are based on hypothetical or simulated investing. We make no representations or warranties that any investor will, or is likely to, achieve profits like those shown, because hypothetical or simulated performance is not indicative of future results.

Don't enter any investment without understanding the worst-case scenarios of that investment. You may lose your entire investment.

Resources:

<u>Internet</u>

https://www.aaii.com/   (Total Financial Education Resource)

https://corporate.americancentury.com/en.html   (Great Mutual Funds)

https://www.bankrate.com/banking/cds/cd-ladder-guide/   (CD Laddering)

https://www.bankrate.com/cd.aspx   (CD rates)

https://www.collegesavings.org/   (College 529 Plan 411)

https://www.computershare.com/us   (Transfer Agent to Purchase Stocks Direct)

https://www.fidelity.com/   (Great Mutual Funds)

https://www.fdic.gov/   (Check that Online Bank is Legit)

https://www.morningstar.com/   (Resource to Research Mutual Funds and Stocks)

https://www.rothira.com/   (Research the Amazing Roth IRA)

https://www.troweprice.com/corporate/en/home.html   (Great Mutual Funds)

https://www.usaa.com/inet/wc/investments-usaa-mutual-funds?akredirect=true

(Great Mutual Funds for Veterans)

https://www.usdebtclock.org/   (National Debt Statistics)

https://investor.vanguard.com/home/   (Great Mutual Funds)

https://about.vanguard.com/who-we-are/a-remarkable-history/founder-Jack-Bogle-tribute/

https://about.vanguard.com/who-we-are/a-remarkable-history/ (Vanguard History)

https://finance.yahoo.com/   (Yahoo Finance)

Chapter 8

Saving and Investing

Summary Questions

Exercise Time: minimum 25 minutes.

As mentioned earlier in this chapter, savings are one of the most important steps in gaining financial freedom. In order to make it a habit, you need to understand its importance. For that, attempt this activity with an open mind. This may have a life-changing impact on you.

I.   *How do you feel about savings? Do you consider savings important?*

II.   *Do you save? If no, what do you think is your biggest obstacle to this simple step (everything's simple once you do it)?*

III.   *What is an ETF? Refer to the reading to help you.*

IV.   *How easy do you find it to save? Do you spend more than you save?*

V.   *Why should you save for an emergency fund? What are the alternatives to having an emergency fund?*

VI.   *Do you pay your credit card balances in full on your credit card monthly?*

Action Plan!

1. Create a paper stock list and complete with your classmates. See

   https://www.investopedia.com/simulator/. Trade for 30 days and see how you do. Use the

   simulator to test your theories about companies you like. It is best to invest in a company

   that you know something about. Do you own an I phone? Research the appropriate stock.

   Watch Netflix? Research the appropriate stock.

2. Find and read about one of the best investors of all time, Warren Buffett. His

   biography is inspiring.

3. Open an account at *www.treasury.gov* and buy an I Bond.

4. If you are a minor ask your guardian to open a custodial account. This means you

   own the account, but your parents are in ultimate control.

Chapter 9

Non-Essential Expenses

The waste of money cures itself, for soon there is no more to waste.

–M.W. Harrison

Introduction

The Average American Spends Almost $18,000 a year on non-essentials, according to an article by the Motley Fool.

Opportunity Cost

When you spend on an unnecessary want, the result is less money available to save and invest. It is necessary for you to save to build wealth. The more money you spend on wants, the less money you save. I call the earnings lost on the money NOT saved and invested opportunity cost.

Chapter Nine: Non-Essential Expenses, considers the many small expenses we justify a million different ways. They make us feel better, look better, or qualify as retail therapy. With a little pre-planning, you can budget these experiences. However, overindulgence results in expenses exceeding income, and the result is a broken budget. What follows is a small list of items that may cause you a problem. As a financial coach, I am just a little confused talking to people who have no emergency funds, no savings, high levels of personal debt, credit card debt, and no equity in their homes that are purchasing the items on the upcoming list before taking care of essentials.

Tattoos

Is this a funny subject for a personal finance book? Wait for it.

Tattoos are very personal decisions. Many people add tattoos to their body for diverse reasons: in tribute, to signify an important person in their life, an event, or just to add an interesting dynamic to one's body. Some folks add stars/constellations, nature themes, tribal themes, faces, religious themes, and animal themes. They can be a status symbol. Human history regarding tattoos is less friendly. In ancient Greece and Rome, tattoos were used to identify slaves. Beginning in the 1800s, circus sideshows displayed tattooed people. To avoid British impressment, sailors tattooed themselves to prove their identity. Military personnel get tattoos to show their social solidarity, give tribute, and tell their story. A friend in medical school told me that in modern emergency room training, tattoos can signify that the patient is the property of another.

Why talk about this in a personal financial book? How much do tattoos cost? A full sleeve tattoo costs around $1,500. Friends, tattoos are expensive. A tattoo is a very expensive piece of artwork that does not increase in value by itself. It is entertainment that does not earn an income or assist you in paying an expense. Life is expensive. Do you have enough discretionary income (money left over after all expenses are paid) to pay for body art?

Let's look at the full picture:

1. Tattoos are expensive. Full sleeve tattoos cost about $1,500. Tattoo artists charge by the hour. The normal rate in my area is between $100 and $125, or more. More for a tattoo artist with a great reputation.

2. They are difficult and time-consuming to apply. The time for an "average difficulty" full sleeve is 10-15 hours. Some complicated full color projects may take 80 hours and entire projects often take multiple sessions, taking time periods of many weeks

or months! Could you use your time more productively? I suggest using this time for creating another income stream.

    a. Tattoos expose you to unnecessary medical risk. Well, Ken, I thought this was a personal finance book, and now you are discussing medical issues. Medical treatment is not free and takes valuable time to administer. Both reasons are financial in scope.

3. Masks skin cancer - A tattoo may hide skin cancer. Suspicious looking moles can hide behind a tattoo design, making it difficult for your dermatologist to inspect your skin for skin cancer.

4. Infection - Getting a tattoo can expose you to harmful bacterial infections.

5. Allergy - You may have an allergy to a particular color or type of ink. Tattoo ink is permanent, so if you find out you are allergic to the ink, it is possible you will suffer allergy symptoms until you remove the ink. You pay again to get the tattoo removed.

6. Some inks are being studied for their potential role in skin cancer. Inks are unregulated.

7. MRI Burning- Tattoos can lead to skin burns when tattooed skin it exposed to MRI scans. It's rare, but do you see the pattern here? There is a lot more going on here than just a pretty design on your "tukis" (rump). In addition, without the possibility of a burn, there

still exists the possibility that your tattoo will distort the MRI image you are trying to get to diagnose some other medical "situation." Don't forget to remove your piercings, too.

8. Affects how you sweat - Doctors have reported tattoos affect how you sweat. Large tattoos don't sound like a good idea. We sweat without interference without an ink coating on our skin.

9. Hepatitis - A dirty needle could pack this bad news.

10. According to research from the International Journal of Dermatology, individuals with tattoos were more likely to be diagnosed with mental health issues and report sleep problems. I'm not sure what comes first, the tattoo or the risky behavior, but the report suggests a relationship between tattoo application and risky behavior.

11. Opens yourself up to unfair prejudice, even though tattoos are mainstream now.

12. Many people who get tattoos end up regretting their decision. Cost of removal is more expensive than the application. Removal may take months and multiple laser sessions. I recommend you hire a physician for the procedure to reduce the risk of unregulated care (more expense). Amateur removal could cause burns and scarring. Each session may cost you $450. Reports show tattoo removal to be more painful than tattoo application. There is pain after the procedure and the site blisters and swells.

Solution: Don't get a tattoo. You look great without it! (Said in strong, but loving teacher voice.)

Home Gym Systems, Computerized Stationary Bikes, Tread Mills, and Gym Memberships

This is a budget item that will exercise your wallet! How about the best computerized stationary bike on the planet? It costs only $58.00 per month for…thirty-nine months! That's $2,262! That does not include the membership fee giving you access to the pretty instructors and your exercise analytics! The membership costs an additional $39.00 per month! Breaking news, 2021 update, now the cost is $64.00 monthly, and the membership is $49 per month!

If you are a rockstar, get two! The alternative here is very realistic and a lot less expensive. Buy a real bike. One that you can ride on a sunny day. For rainy days and winter weather, purchase a "trainer" stand that converts your bike into a stationary/spin bike for $90.00. I found one on Amazon. Then set your bike in front of your TV and watch whatever you want! No extra charge! I saved you over $2,100!

Home gyms cost from $1,000 to $2,000. If this is your thing, fine. Most people who buy a home gym system or treadmill end up not using them. This makes sense. The machines are big and bulky, and it's not a lot of fun exercising alone in your home.

An alternative is to take up the right sport. Take up a sport that is fun, promotes exercise, and is entertaining. Tennis is a good sport and inexpensive to start. Many local parks have tennis courts. Many companies sponsor ball teams. If you live in a winter wonderland, try bowling. Jogging is an inexpensive sport. Yes, each of these sports has a small expense, but budget them under health, entertainment and social.

If you are not interested in any of these ideas, just walk; 10,000 or more steps a day is a significant form of exercise. The creator made us for walking!

Gym memberships often wind up as recurring charges on your credit card. We often forget recurring charges. This is what I call gray charges. These are subscription charges to your credit card that have been forgotten because we are not checking our credit card statement monthly. Your gym company will forget to give you a courtesy call reminding you to cancel.

Twenty percent of Americans go to gyms.

Most people don't make it past the five-month mark. Only half of the members go regularly.

Defaulted gym membership contracts can be a cloud on your credit report. When I was selling real-estate, I was assisting a client pre-qualify for a loan. He had an unpaid gym membership, and that was enough for our favorite lender to refuse mortgage pre-approval.

CrossFit can be more expensive than gym memberships. Average prices range from $75.00 to $225.00 per month.

Solution: Run or walk on your own for the simplest, least expensive form of exercise. For weight training, find the least expensive local gym.

Home Food Delivery

Home Food Delivery cost is another unforced error to your budget and wallet.

It is five times more expensive to order delivery from a restaurant than to cook from home. Meal kit delivery services are three times more expensive than cooking from scratch at home. You pay more money for convenience. I know it takes effort to prepare home-cooked meals, but regardless, you can still prepare home-cooked meals.

According to Wellio, the average price per meal in a restaurant is $20.37, the meal kit is $12.53, and home cooking is $4.31.

Boats

"A boat is a hole in the water surrounded by wood in which to pour money." –Anonymous.

"The two happiest days of a man's life—the day he bought the boat and the day he sold the boat," *Anonymous*

B.O.A.T.: Break Out Another Thousand (dollars).

See where this is going? I have had a lot of fun on boats. They are amazing entertainment. I live in Florida and water surrounds this great state. You cannot see the "real" Florida without getting on the water by boat. That does not give you permission to spend tens of thousands of dollars when a tour boat will do. I have owned two boats in my life, and I paid cash. Borrowing money to buy a boat is not a good idea. They depreciate faster than cars and have no practical purpose. At least I can drive my depreciating automobile to work.

Boating is fun. Most boaters enjoy boating to relax, go fishing, and spend time with family. If you went fishing or boating as a child, you are more likely to become a lifelong boater. According to the NMMA, 142 million Americans went Boating in 2016. During the pandemic, boating became more popular, as Americans looked for alternatives to sitting at home watching the news.

From an older report, the middle class enjoys boating with an average annual income of $100,000. In 2019, average boat prices ranged from $600 to the stratosphere. The average price for a boat is around $20,000. That is from my personal experience.

My point here is that if you are going through a financially tough time, boating should be out of the picture until you are out of your financial situation.

My last "interesting" experience was with my father's last boat. He financed the new boat. It was bought at full price from the showroom floor in 2007 at the time the economy was reaching the top of the bubble of the Financial Crisis. The boat's price was about $50,000; $20,000 put down (money from selling the previous boat) and financed $30,000. In 2 years, he was upside down in the boat (figuratively) meaning the money for the down payment, or his equity disappeared. (In a boat? Equity?) Dad stored the boat at a marina, albeit an inexpensive one, incurring further expense. Membership in Sea Tow (the boat equivalent of AAA) is another expense. Dad paid additional principal payments on the note to stay financially afloat. Did I mention the expense of accessories? When you buy a new boat, there are additional expenses to consider. Boats need line, anchors, lifejackets, electronics (expensive), spare parts, a spare battery, a tool kit, a first aid kit, and on and on.

When dad turned 80, he ended his carefree days of boating. (Actually, boats require a lot of care.) We sold the boat to an investor who shipped the boat to England because this style of boat was popular there.

Instead, if you love boats like I do, consider a boat rental club. They give you several boats to choose from; you pick up the boat at the marina and return the boat later in the day. The marina cleans and maintains it. You don't have to worry about the expensive accessories. If you want to own a boat or have a boat, I offer a few tips: most thrifty boaters do their own boat maintenance.

My outboard is very easy to maintain. It's not rocket science, but boat maintenance is expensive if you always take your boat to the shop. Have a place to store your boat free of cost. Marina storage or outdoor storage lots are expensive. I store my boat in my yard.

Clean your own boat. I made a lot of money as a teenager cleaning boats belonging to the wealthy. It's expensive to pay for someone else to clean your boat. I take my boat to a freshwater lake, jump in, and clean the above water parts of the boat while floating on the lake!

Learn how to pilot your boat and don't boat under the influence. Check out the US Coast Guard Auxiliary http://www.cgaux.org/boatinged/ for boating courses near you. Boating involves a lot of moving parts and ignorance here can be costly.

RV Life

Driving to work each day, I pass by an outdoor storage facility filled with RVs that are just stored. They never move! Their owners never seem to use them. Why? Why did good folks buy these RVs and never use them?

The Boat and RV Storage Graveyard

Owning a "live aboard" size RV during retirement may be a way to save money and be on vacation full time! Owning an RV to sit in your yard or incur additional expense stored in a storage yard is not good for your budget.

According to https://www.rvia.org, ten million households own an RV. The typical RV owner is forty-eight years old, married, and earns an annual household income of $62,000. They spend three to four weeks in their RV.

Solution: Try renting an RV before buying.

Check out https://gorving.com/.

RV's run the gamut of price. A pop-up camper starts at $5,000 while a class one motorhome costs over $200,000. My in-laws RVd full time in their retirement and they had a blast. They were very thrifty. You can afford to have a nice RV if you sold the ranch! See https://roadslesstraveled.us/rv-budget/ to research the full-time lifestyle.

Do not buy an RV on a romantic whim, store it in an outdoor storage lot, and then forget it. That's a waste of money. We do not own stuff. Stuff owns us. RV expenses include gas, insurance, maintenance, and campsite rent. Plan and create a budget to keep this hobby in perspective.

Cable before Dishonor!

Americans love to sit at home and order food online and binge watch their favorite show, also streaming online. On average, Americans spend approximately $23 monthly for TV streaming and/or an additional $90 per month for cable. My suggestion is that you shop wisely and hold your service provider accountable to the level of service your provider promised. I check my internet speed to make sure I'm getting the horsepower I'm promised. Make sure your bill is accurate. Use a service like Ask Trim https://www.asktrim.com/ to renegotiate your fees. Most Americans can save money by cutting the cable connection and relying solely on streaming services, called Paid Per View, on their TV. When you cut the cable, you can expect to save about $100 per month.

My personal story: While my children were home, we did not have cable. Streaming TV did not exist. We had dial-up internet for most of that time. I paid about $15/month for the Internet and somehow, we survived. We had rabbit ears on our TV to pick up the local channels and when those signals changed to digital, I purchased a digital amplifier and continued to use my 'rabbit ears.' Yes, I am an oddball. An oddball who saved, in my estimate, about $12,000 in cable fees during that time frame.

My point is to consider cutting the cable and use a Payment on Demand (POD) service like Amazon Prime, ROKU or Apple TV.

In fact, you can stream a lot of content free! Another perk is these services do not ask for a credit card number! There are a few conditions, but free streaming is something to consider. Here are a few key takeaways. Make sure you have the right equipment, like a ROKU or Amazon Firestick, ,and a strong internet connection. Be ready to see commercials. That is the tradeoff to a free service like Crackle or IMDb. You won't have access to the latest and greatest content, but you will have more selections than time to watch. So, check out the following free streaming services and save a ton of money! I use Crackle, FreeVee and Vudu. I am thrilled with their services.

1. Vudu;
2. Crackle;
3. FreeVee TV;
4. Roku Channel;
5. Popcornflix;
6. Kanopy;

One-Third of Americans Spend More on Coffee than in Investing.

This is the headline from a 2018 fool.com article. Obviously, a sound bite, but their data comes from the Acorns 2017 Money Matters Report that used a SurveyMonkey survey. They surveyed 3,010 Americans, women and males between the ages of eighteen and forty-four. I thought the above comment was because we invested so few dollars. According to this survey, the sample group spent over $1,000 per year on coffee. That's $2.74 per day. That's easy to do at Starbucks. My take is that most Americans spend $5.00 per week, or $250/yr. A survey conducted by Accounting Principals in 2013 reported that 82% of the American work force spend $20 per week or $1,040 per year. Younger workers spent more than older workers. Maybe the older workers were saving for retirement.

We have a love affair with coffee. I like coffee. You like coffee. We all like coffee. **Solution:** I brew my coffee at home, put into a travel mug, and off to work I go. Simple, easy, and cheap.

Buying Lunch Out

According to a popular survey by Accounting Principals that surveyed 1,000 American workers, it was discovered that respondents paid over $36.00 per week or $1,800 per year for lunch. Another more recent source reports workers spend $173 per month for lunch. That gets us over $2,000 per year.

Solution: Time to learn what a brown bag is. I pack a lunch daily and only eat out on special occasions. Try coordinating eating out with the freebies restaurants offer customers for birthdays and other special events.

Rideshare - Uber/Lyft

Estimates differ, but seems the "average" American spends between $50 and $100 per month for ridesharing. If you are on business and you will get reimbursed, that's fine. If you need to get across the street because it is raining, well that's just silly, buy an umbrella. I've heard stories of teens hailing Ubers to get to school. Buy a bike. Take the bus.

However, if you want to sell your family's second car to save expenses, then car sharing services could save you money as an alternative.

Sports Season and Music Concerts

I just received a flyer for a concert being held in my hometown. Our fair city has a great venue with 6,000 seats. I looked at the ticket prices and almost fainted! I believe I may understand why. According to an article reported by the Economist magazine, as soon as they release music concert tickets, a subsidiary of the "band" buys and resells the tickets at a higher price than face value to enrich the pockets of the "band." It means that the artists scalp their own tickets! Live Nation, a concert promoter, admitted to this in July 2019. The artists turnaround and blame legit scalpers, managers, and agents. The artists did not want to appear greedy by their beloved fans. Promoters design venue premium memberships and verified fan programs to move as much money from your pocket to theirs.

This recent development of "taking you to the cleaners" is for the changing role of the concert. It is now the major income producer for the artist since sales of albums have disappeared. If you like an expensive music concert scene, I hope you are an heiress, because you will need to be to keep up this expensive habit.

Wedding Expenses

The cost of a wedding does not predict its future success!

A friend told me that after announcing her engagement, wedding vendors, dentists and gyms came out of the woodwork to sell her unnecessary services. Remember, money doesn't care who it belongs to. As a reformed wedding photographer, I have seen countless brides and their families rack up enormous expenses getting ready for the wedding day. According to the Knot, the average cost of an American wedding was $33,000 in 2019. Holy smokes! Be careful of the Wedding Industrial Complex. I find these figures "interesting." I suspect wedding expenses will return to pre-COVID highs as the pandemic moves further away in the rear-view mirror. Parents are financing weddings. If invested over time, such funds could grow into a significant nest egg. I am sure that you can find an inexpensive wedding venue if you look hard enough. If your wedding will be a "show off" event to your friends and family, well, God Bless. Have fun spending that money. One bride's mom told me, after the wedding, upon my delivery of the photos, that she spent more money on alcohol than on photography! Because of my experience of photographing weddings, I am sure I could plan one. I know I could create a budget for one. I photographed a wedding at a state park. You can buy wedding gowns pre-owned! Research, then shop for Flowers, Photography, DJs, and Caterers before deciding. KEEP IT SIMPLE!

Wedding Party Expense

Has your friend asked you to be a bridesmaid or groomsmen in a wedding? Congratulations. This social obligation expense can be a budget wrecker. Is a bachelorette or bachelor cruise or other obligatory pre-wedding festivities necessary? That can add up to $1,000. This is one of the latest fads in pre-marriage traditions. "Cruising for a financial bruising," bridesmaids spend $500 to $1,000 for a bachelorette cruise. Can you afford that? Dresses cost, well, whatever the bride expects. I hope your bride is frugal and does not expect the world of you.

Funerals: Again, if you have enough money, spend the national average of $7,000-$10,000 for a funeral. These fees include services at the funeral home, burial in a cemetery, and headstone installation. Cremation costs half. It is possible to do a direct cremation with no ceremony for less than $1,000. It is possible to buy cremation in advance and save even more. But, be careful if you prepay! Make sure you are dealing with a reputable company that is not going out of business before the death of your loved one. What if you move to an area not served by your funeral agency? If you cannot afford an expensive funeral, consider purchasing a small life/final expense insurance policy of $5,000-$10,000.

"If you have debt, I'm willing to bet that general clutter is a problem for you too." –Suze Orman

I agree with Suze here. Americans used to keep their cars in their garages. According to the US Department of Energy survey, 25% of people with two-car garages don't park in them at all. A third of respondents reported they can only park one car due to garage clutter. About 9% of Americans rent storage space, even though 65% of those homeowners have a garage (Self-Storage Association stat). Even though a large percentage of homes have three-car garages, I still see most of my neighbors parking their vehicles in their driveway because their garage is full of clutter. Is it possible to fit two cars into a two-car garage in 2022??

Self-Storage Unit

Step 1: Get a new Credit Card

Step 2: Rent a Self-Storage Unit.

Step 3: Pack it full of worthless stuff while paying $100 a month in storage fees!

Renting a self-storage unit for short-term temporary storage of the valuable heirloom furniture during the moving process may be suitable if finding the perfect residence in your new location is taking longer than expected. However, as soon as you have found your new abode, clean out the self-storage unit. Try to use the storage unit for less than three months. They are a tremendous financial drain and encourage collecting and storing material goods that are NOT being used. Sell them. Give them away! Several sources call self-storage units a sad museum of personal failure, which is filled with unfinished projects, unwanted furniture, and unnecessary clutter. **Again, said in loving teacher's voice!**

SOLUTION: Buy a shed. In my family, we always had a cheap steel shed in the backyard. It was a kit, and you built it yourself. If you are not a kit friendly person, buy an affordable "plastic" shed from your favorite home improvement retailer.)

Video Game Subscriptions

Video gaming is a big attraction, and you should know the complete cost of a subscription. The gaming industry is a turn style built on planned obsolescence. Once you enter particular gaming companies' "environments," you will be encouraged to purchase expensive updated hardware and pay a monthly subscription price that you have no control over.

Video game subscriptions range from $10 to $20 per month, and that does not include the cost of the PC or gaming controller.

Assorted, possibly unnecessary, subscription packages that can be budget busters.

Subscription Boxes	Monthly Fee
Stitch Fix	$20 Styling Fee, Expensive Clothes
Trunk Club	$25 Styling Fee
Dollar Shave	Up to $9.00 monthly
Harry's	About $80/year
Blue Apron	$10.00 per meal
Hot Sauce of the Month	$12.00 per month
Craft Beer Club	$40.00 monthly

Personal Grooming

Women enjoy the benefits of spending big bucks on a hairdo. Haircare sources estimate women spend $55,000 in a lifetime on hair care.

The average nail care cost in the US is $1,345 per year.

The cost of manicures, pedicures, haircuts, and blow-outs cost you $1,797 per year.

This may be a great place to save money and get your budget back in line!

Gifts

According to the National Retail Federation and a Gallup Poll in 2018, Americans will spend $885 on Christmas gifts. Here is another great budget buster. Put this item in your budget and stick to it. Your children will not love you anymore if you don't buy them stuff! America spends over $40 billion dollars on games and toys. That is more than many of those same Americans saved and invested! Americans spent a record $16 billion on Father's Day or $139 per person. Mother's Day earned $25 billion or $195 per person. The average wedding gift is

$118. Don't keep up with appearances if you are on a tight budget. Consider thoughtful handmade gifts. Do you craft? Are you a carpenter? I always appreciate a handmade gift. Never go into debt to keep up with mega consumers.

Inexpensive Hobbies

When you have downtime, try to spend your time wisely by finding free things to do. Check your local free newspaper or community website to see what free events are happening in your area. Consider reading a book on a topic that interests you. Listen to podcasts. Consider using your free time to volunteer. Check with a local church or check out Habitat for Humanity. Volunteering gives you a double whammy. You find an activity that is free while getting a good feeling helping others. If that is not a win-win, I don't know what is.

In Conclusion:

I know this section is stressful and complicated. It is important to talk about these unnecessary expenses because our economy and culture encourage us to spend more than we should on these goods and services. The people that provide these services are good people making a living providing a service they love to do. That is okay. What is not okay is overspending. Before deciding to spend on an unnecessary good or service, please consult your budget. You will be happy you did after the excitement, passion and emotion of the purchase fades. Another great tip is to wait a week and see if you are still passionate about the new purchase.

Chapter 9

Non-Essential Expenses

Summary Questions

Exercise Time: approximately 15 minutes.

Time for a little self-analysis. The more you know about your behavior, the better you will be able to control yourself. In order to help you identify your behavior, try answering these questions with a rational mind, zero emotions, and 100% honesty.

I.	*What does over-spending look and sound like to you? Define an over-spender.*

II.	*Do you spend without considering the full cost? If yes, what makes you do so?*

III.	*Do you know anyone whose life or career was ruined their career just because they spent more than they earned?*

IV.	*Do you buy items that are not in your budget?*

V.	*Do you make impulse purchases with your credit card? If yes, what were your purchases? Did you later suffer from Buyer's Remorse?*

VI.   *List creative ways you consider making purchases. Research the Ben Franklin*

        method for deciding.

VII. Do you consider less expensive alternatives for entertainment or are you in the

      FOMO, Fear of Missing Out Crowd?

A brief assignment!

Think of all the enormous or large expenses you have made in the past 2 years. Ask your group leader to share their experiences with large purchases. Try to recall as many as you can. Make down a list of them and then check those you later discovered as useless. Now, what's the total amount of money you wasted in the past 2 years?

Write it down!!! Discuss it!!!

Chapter 10

DUIs and Other Legal Calamities

"A Tree Never Hits an automobile except in self-defense."

–Woody Allen

DUIs themselves are not a financial concept. DUI has severe financial consequences. Please use the following information to avoid the financial, legal, and emotional turmoil associated with DUI.

Driving drunk is no joke because drunk driving ruins so many innocent lives. There is no excuse. Over 1.4 million arrests for DUI per year occur according to the National Highway Traffic Administration. According to MADD, Mothers Against Drunk Driving, drunk driving costs the American economy $132 billion per year. Twenty-eight people die every day in the United States because of alcohol related deaths.

The total cost of getting a DUI for the first time in the state of Florida is between $7,500 and $10,000. The Florida amount is similar to the national average. The average time to settle your DUI case is five months. The second DUI will cost almost the same as the first, and the percentage of people convicted on the second offense is higher. This increases your chance of receiving a sentence that includes jail time. It is my understanding that it can be pretty difficult to keep a job and still fulfill a jail sentence at the same time.

Speaking of jobs, I know for a fact that financial services companies will not hire prospects if they have a felony DUI. A felony DUI says something about your character that may prevent you from certain "driving unrelated" careers.

Prepare for your auto insurance premium to skyrocket. The auto insurance premium increase alone is between $3,300 and $6,000 (after you get your driving privilege back). A friend just told me her insurance rate after one DUI was $5,000 per 6 months in Florida. In Florida, you must acquire an SR-22, a document that allows you to reinstate your license after purchasing pricey auto insurance. The SR-22, in Florida, has to be in place for three years before you can buy insurance without one. The repeat DUI or DWI offender has to acquire FR-44 insurance. Some say FR-44 is "DUI" insurance. The restrictions are stricter than the SR-22. For instance, if there is a lapse of coverage, the three-year term resets to when you reinstate. Leaving the state of Florida does not help your situation. You also must pay the premium six months at a time, as there are no convenient monthly payments. According to MADD, 50-75% of convicted DUI offenders continue to drive with a suspended license. You can hire a high-powered, experienced (read expensive) lawyer to request an administrative hearing with your state's Department of Motor Vehicles to appeal the loss of your driver's license.

So, besides a large part of your savings and income now being committed to paying your debt to society, you may also rely on others to get back and forth from work. If your job requires you to have a driver's license, you'll be looking for a new job on your bicycle! This is another area where your finances will suffer from the DUI. Your ability to make a living may change.

After getting your driving privileges back, you may need to install an ignition (interlock) safety switch that checks your breath every time you drive to abide by the law. That should begin great conversations with your young children in the car. An Interlock Ignition Safety Switch costs $500-$1,500.

Court ordered alcohol treatment classes? $500 - $1,000.

Probation Supervision: $1,000.

According to dui.drivinglaws.org, your total first time Florida DUI experience may include the following:

1. License Suspension

2. Jail Time

3. Fines

4. Probation

5. Community Service

6. Ignition Interlock Device

7. Vehicle Impoundment

Florida law requires you to take a breath, blood, or urine test if arrested for DUI. It's called "implied consent" and it's on your Florida driver's license. You agreed to it. Check your state laws regarding your home state.

Here is a subject where I believe you should learn from "other" people's mistakes! The poor choice of driving under the influence could ruin your life!

The next time you need a ride after drinking, call a taxicab, a Lyft, or an Uber.

Chapter 10

DUIs and Other Legal Calamities

Summary Questions

Exercise Time: minimum 10 minutes.

I. *When is it acceptable to drive while you're drunk or under the influence?*

II. *In your opinion, is there an acceptable amount of alcohol that you can drink and still drive safely? If there is, would you consider drinking an acceptable amount of alcohol before driving?*

III. *Explain the consequences of not having enough money to pay the court-ordered classes, fines, and attorney fees?*

IV.   What happens when you lose your driver's license? Do you lose your driving

privileges?

V.   Do you know of real-life accidents that occurred because of drunk driving? If not,

Google recent DUI incidents in your area.

One Last Activity!

Now that you have answered all the above questions, discuss with the class any thoughts or insights you have regarding driving while impaired. Is drinking and driving worth the hassle of losing your driving privileges, being exposing you to enormous insurance rates, risking your life, and risking the lives of other innocent people?

Specifically, research employers that disallow employment, even unrelated to driving, if you have a DUI felony on your record.

I hope you enjoyed your Get WalletWise adventure. There are many lessons to learn from this text, and it may take a few years to master them. Remember to enter any contract slowly and with your eyes wide open. From the old movie, *Indiana Jones*, choose wisely when deciding. Don't forget to check out www.walletwise.org for additional resources.